Robin Williams **Design** Workshop
Second Edition

Robin Williams **Design** Workshop
Second Edition

Robin Williams   **John Tollett**

Published by Peachpit Press • Berkeley • California

Robin Williams Design Workshop, second edition
Robin Williams and John Tollett

Peachpit Press
1249 Eighth Street
Berkeley, California 94710
800.283.9444
510.524.2178
510.524.2221 fax

Find us on the web at **www.peachpit.com**
To report errors, please send a note to errata@peachpit.com
Peachpit Press is a division of Pearson Education

A number of logos were designed by Landon Dowlen of Landonsea Design, www.Landonsea.com. Many of the web sites in Chapter 11 were designed by Brian Forstat of AgilityGraphics.com, Landon Dowlen of Landonsea.com, LStudio.net, DNAcommunications.com, and RothRitter.com. We have great appreciation for all!

Cover design and production by John Tollett
Interior design by Robin Williams and John Tollett
Interior production by Robin Williams
Index by Barbara Sikora
Editing by Nancy Davis
Prepress by David Van Ness

ISBN
0-321-44176-1

10 9 8 7 6 5 4 3 2 1

Printed and bound in the United States of America

Contents

It must be nice . . .

Clip Art
Stock Images
Posters Contrast
Web Sites

SUBS 2 GO

MEET SOCCER SUPERSTAR
JAY BAYKAL!

20

FRIDAY 6PM
Register to win a soccer ball autographed by Jay "The Turk" Baykal!

Letterheads
Brochures
Invoices
Indices Newsletters
Cerrillos Echo
Ads
Flyers Envelopes
Business Cards
Billboards
Explore Logos Forms
Tables of Contents
Visual Impact

Aren't you sick of hearing comments like these: "It must be nice to sit around all day just being creative." "Lucky you, you get to have fun instead of working." Meanwhile you're up all night sweating out a deadline for a big meeting tomorrow morning, your mind is a blank, and the clock is moving faster than usual. Or, even worse, this job could be your big break and if you score big on this project you'll have more work than you need. Now, why does that design look boring?

If you've never been there it's probably because you're a living-legend genius designer and you've never had to deal with the fears, inadequacies, insecurities, paranoia, and limitations of us mere-mortal designers. And if that's true, you're most likely not reading this book anyway.

If you are a mere-mortal designer, welcome, and it's nice to know that we (Robin and I) are not alone. By "mere-mortal designers" I mean aspiring designers who are in the process of developing their skills and getting experience; designers who are not famous (yet); and designers who are looking for design books to add to their collection, books that will give them some insight into the design process.

Hey, what a coincidence! That's who we had in mind when we wrote and designed this book. It's our hope that the practical approach we use in design will be helpful to you and the way you approach graphic design projects. With the fantastic digital tools and resources available to you, the only thing separating you from the top designers in the world is the opportunity to unleash your imagination on the world. That and a few mega-buck clients, but that could happen, too.

We've attempted to communicate a spirit of playful design exploration and experimentation in the examples we've used and in the design of the book itself. That playfulness and a willingness to experiment visually can open the door to your imagination. And it can transform a stressful assignment into a satisfying creative exercise.

We all have a tendency to revert to completely safe design solutions that we know will work when we're under the pressure of a deadline, such as using the font Helvetica and designing with a centered alignment. This book encourages you to explore beyond that and to have fun doing it. The examples here are meant to help spark ideas and steer your creative thinking in different directions that might lead to previously unseen possibilities in your own work.

We'd like for this book to add to your future enjoyment of being a designer. But most of all, we'd like for you to say "Oh, I don't work. I just sit around playing all day."

jt + rw

A CONVERSATION WITH CRITICS

"We all revere the genius Bach;
  Each contrapuntal law,
  Each voice and phrase that interlock
  Inspires a sense of awe."

"Quite right. Chopin we also praise.
  Such drama, and such sweep!
  Each time I hear that Polonaise
  It almost makes me weep."

"Rachmaninoff! He knew the deeps
  To which a soul can sink.
  To wit, his Third Concerto keeps
  Me busy trying to think."

> *But Anderson; now there's style!*
> *He's got them beat by half;*
> *His music always makes me smile,*
> *And often makes me laugh.*

"How plebian that comment was!
  Let this be understood:
  If that is what his music does,
  It can't be any good."

ROSS CARTER, KENTUCKY POET
Evensong · poems

GOONHAVERN PRESS

Some designers
are equally inept
at following rules
or breaking them.
Good designers
can do either.

Jim Alley
Savannah College of Art and Design

Typefaces used in this chapter:
Headlines: Barmeno Extra Bold
Body copy: Clearface Regular and **Heavy**
*This combination of softly rounded sans serif
with a classic oldstyle (tending toward the slab
serif style) creates an informal, grammar-
school look to this chapter.*

1. How Much Do You Already Know?

separations
duotone
SCREEN FONT
OpenType
resolution
dpi
raster
registration
Process Color
Spot Color
moiré
PostScript
PRINTER FONT
native file format
KERNING
EPS
TrueType
halftone
suitcase
JPEG
line Screen
ppi
VECTOR
TRACKING
alias
GIF
screen font
anti-alias
RGB
CMYK
registration
TIFF

In this section we want to make sure you have the basic building blocks down before we launch into more advanced concepts. You can certainly learn a lot from *this* book even if you don't have the basics down yet. But to move forward, we have to assume you know certain things. Since Robin has already written a number of books for new designers, this introduction is sort of a touchstone; if you can't answer the questions, we refer you to books that you might want to read. And the questions are not just about design, but about all the things designers now have to know to produce our work, all the technical stuff we need to deal with to get our jobs done properly.

Most of the books we recommend are in the "Non-Designer's" series. Perhaps you are already a designer and discover there are things in the Non-Designer's books that you need to learn, but you just can't bring yourself to buy a book for "non-designers." Well, have your mother buy it and send it to you wrapped in brown paper. Paste a photo over the cover so no one knows you own "that" book. Rip the cover off. Or just get over yourself. And lighten up! All of us have more to learn, no matter what level we think we are at right now.

What are the basic Principles?

Can you put into words why one design "works" and another doesn't? Can you explain to a client why their dorky design idea doesn't project the professional level of their service and why your new improved version does? When you look at a poorly designed page, can you **put into words** why it looks amateurish, and can you put into words what needs to be done to make it look more sophisticated? Being able to explain concepts in words helps you pinpoint problems, find solutions more quickly, and convince clients of your superior design skills.

1. Can you name at least five reasons why the flyer below looks amateurish?

> **CHESS MATCH**
>
> **SUNDAY, AUGUST 23**
>
> **MEET IN COMMU-NITY ROOM AT 3:00 P.M.**
>
> **SPECIAL GUEST-KRAMNIK!**

2. From glancing at the typical business card layout below, how can you tell it came from one of those sample books in the local copy shop?

> Amy Meilander   Robin Williams
>
> *THE UNDERSTANDERS*
>
> www.TheUnderstanders.com
> (505) 555-5555

If you cannot answer the questions on these two pages easily, you need to read the first half of *The Non-Designer's Design Book*.

3. Compare these two layouts. They are both centered, but one looks more sophisticated than the other. What changes were made to the one on the right to give it this higher-quality look, even though it is still a centered arrangement?

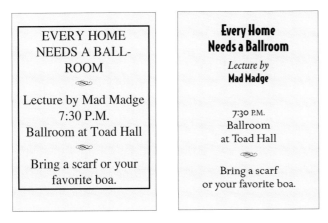

5. Glance at these two layouts. Which one do your find your eye is naturally attracted to? What is the word for the design principle that attracts your eye in this case, and how was it achieved?

4. In the example below, which simple principle can be applied that would instantly give it a more professional appearance?

SKATERS WEEKLY

VOLUME 43	ISSUE 7

**Guilty Looks
Enter Tree Beers**

Wants pawn term dare worsted ladle gull hoe hat search putty yowler coils debt pimple colder Guilty Looks.

Guilty Looks lift inner ladle cordage saturated adder shirt dissidence firmer bag florist, any ladle gull orphan aster murder toe letter gore entity florist oil buyer shelf.

"Guilty Looks!" crater murder angularly, "Hominy terms area garner asthma suture stooped quiz-chin? Goiter door florist? Sordidly nut!"

"Wire nut, murder?" wined Guilty Looks, hoe dint peony tension tore murder's dilly scaldings.

"Cause dorsal lodge a wicket beer inner florist hoe orphan molasses pimple. Ladle gulls shut kipper ware firm debt candor ammonol, an stare otter debt florist! Debt florist's mush toe dentures furry ladle gull!"

Wail, pimple oil-wares wander doe wart udder pimple dum wampum toe doe. Debt's jest

hormone nurture. Wan moaning, Guilty Looks dissipater murder, an win entity florist.

An Avengeress Gull

Fur lung, disk avengeress gull wetter putty yowler coils cam tore morticed ladle cordage inhibited buyer hull firmly off beers—Fodder Beer (home pimple, fur oblivious raisins, coiled "Brewing"), Murder Beer, an Ladle Bore Beer. Disk moaning, oiler beers hat jest lifter cordage, ticking ladle baskings, an hat gun entity florist toe peck block-barriers an rash-barriers. Guilty Looks ranker dough ball; bought, off curse, nor-bawdy worse hum, soda sully ladle gull win

baldly rat entity beer's horse!

Honor tipple inner darning rum, stud tree boils fuller sop—wan grade bag boiler sop, wan muddle-sash boil, an wan tawny ladle boil. Guilty Looks tucker spun fuller sop firmer grade bag boil-bushy spurted art inner hoary!

"Archl" crater gull, "Debt sop's toe hart—barns mar tome!"

Dingy traitor sop inner

Ladle limbs

Marry hatter ladle limb
Marry hatter ladle limb
Itch fleas worse widest snore.
An ever-wear debt Marry win
Door limb worse shorter gore.

How is your Typography?

Graphic design is type. If there is no type on the piece, it is not graphic design—it's fine art. Every designer needs to have a thorough understanding of type and typography. You might have a brilliant layout and great copy and a gorgeous photograph, and someone might even have paid you lots of money for it, but if your apostrophes look like they came off a typewriter and you've got two spaces after periods, you're not as good as you think. Long ago designers didn't have to worry about things like where the apostrophe belongs and whether a question mark belongs inside or outside of quotation marks because the professional typesetter did that, but now every designer has to know those details as well as design.

1. Quickly name five serious typographic problems in the sentence below.

   "Oh my gosh", cried Moll.   She gasped--her enigma was all wrapped up in Bob's integrity.

2. What is typographically wrong with each of the phrases below?

   Open 3-6 A.M. every day.

   Closed May-June.

   The San Francisco-New York flight.

3. How do you type these symbols: ® ™ ¢ © •

4. How do you set accent marks, as in the words résumé or voilà?

5. Does a period belong inside or outside of parentheses? What do you do with the punctuation that comes directly after an italic or bold word? When does "its" have an apostrophe? Which typographic marks belong in the blank spaces in this phrase: rock _n_ roll?

6. Name five typographic problems in the column below.

   Lorper adip endreetum velis niamcorem vulputpat irit nim dolenit dolorer alissis nonulputem.

   Lore doloborti iscidunt ulputem verci blandrem ing euipsum incipis nosto do core tatum iriure, od doleniam velit ip exerat. Ut lamet nibh ea Faci Blandre Veliscill mconummy nibh el ex et, veliquatue molorero odolorting ercilit at atis adiamet dipit ute magnim zzriliquisl eugiatie enim ver in vulputet breat.

   Lorperil el ulla cor susto odipisl zzril ing euiscidunt wis nonsequi esent ullam quam ver at, cor senis ad tationulputpatie mod tem deliquamconum quissi.

If you cannot answer these questions, read *The Mac is not a typewriter* or *The PC is not a typewriter*. It's a little book.

1. Match the category of type in the left column to a representative sample in the right column.

Slab serif	*a heap o' livin'*
Sans serif	**keep the thumbmarks**
Oldstyle	ye've got to sing and dance
Modern	yer soul is sort of wrapped
Decorative	**a heap of sun**
Script	*watch beside a loved one*

2. Can you name the problems with the type combinations shown below? How could you make the images stronger?

3. What does the paragraph on the left have that the paragraph on the right does not? What does this technique achieve?

There are three important **rules of life** that will help you survive most situations. **One** is that your attitude is your life. **Two** is that you are what you take the time to become. And **three** is that you can't let the seeds stop you from enjoying the watermelon.

There are three important rules of life that will help you survive most situations. One is that your attitude is your life. Two is that you are what you take the time to become. And three is that you can't let the seeds stop you from enjoying the watermelon.

If you cannot answer the questions above, read the second half of *The Non-Designer's Design Book.*

1. What's the difference between letterspacing, kerning, pair kerning, auto kerning, manual kerning, range kerning, and tracking, and how do you use each of these in your software?

2. What must be done to the quotation below to improve it typographically?

> "Preparation works much better than optimism."

3. Glance at the two paragraphs below. Which one feels easier to read, especially if it was not just a paragraph, but a whole page? State three reasons why. Without changing the typeface, what can be done to the other paragraph to make it as readable as possible?

The tombstone said that everybody loved Mabel. Not me. I adored her. I worshipped her. I wanted to be just like Mabel. I wanted her life and her clothes and her attitude and her kindness and her money. I really wanted her money.

The tombstone said that everybody loved Mabel. Not me. I adored her. I worshipped her. I wanted to be just like Mabel. I wanted her life and her clothes and her attitude and her kindness and her money. I really wanted her money.

If you cannot answer the questions above, read *The Non-Designer's Type Book.*

How is your Color Theory?

Once upon a time a graphic designer had to worry about only one sort of color, CMYK. Now because we are manipulating images on our computers, placing them on web pages, and printing them to desktop color inkjet printers as well as to high-end offset presses, we have to understand color in all of its variations through the processes, and we must know which color model to choose not only for the end result, but for the steps along the way.

1. What does **CMYK** stand for?

2. What does **RGB** stand for?

3. When do you want to **use** CMYK images and when do you want to use RGB images?

4. When would you **scan** an image in CMYK vs. RGB?

5. What happens on the screen when you **change the color mode** from RGB to CMYK?

6. What is **bit depth**? How does it affect the printed image?

7. How does the **pixel-per-inch** count (**ppi**, sometimes referred to as **dpi**) affect an image displayed on a screen, as on a web page? That is, will a 300 ppi image look better on the screen than a 72 ppi image?

8. How can you improve the **resolution** on your monitor?

If you cannot answer these questions, you might want to read *From Design into Print: Preparing Graphics and Text for Print,* **by Sandee Cohen.**

What about Printing?

In this book we might use some of the terms found in these questions. We have to assume that, if you bought this advanced design book, you know what we are talking about if we say something like "notice the moiré pattern," "the halftone screen is too coarse," or "call the printer and find out what lpi they want to use." Not knowing these sorts of things will not prevent you from using and learning from this book! We just want you to know where you can get that information if you discover you need it.

If you cannot answer these questions and want to know all about printing and production so your great designs look great in print, read *From Design into Print: Preparing Graphics and Text for Print,* **by Sandee Cohen.**

1. Is this book **printed** in three-color, four-color, five-color, or full-color?

2. What is **spot color**?

3. What is **process color**?

4. How do the **dots-per-inch (dpi)** affect an image printed on a page? That is, will a 300 dpi image look better in print than a 72 dpi image, even if they are both full color?

5. What is a **linescreen**? How does **lpi** affect a printed image?

6. What is a **halftone**?

7. What is a **duotone** and how do you make one?

8. What is a **moiré** pattern? Why do you want to avoid it? How can you avoid it?

9. What are **separations**?

10. What is a **color tint**?

11. What is the color **registration** and when would you use it?

12. Is the flyer shown below a one-, two-, or three-color job? How many **ink colors** did the designer have to pay for?

Poetry Reading
Mad Madge

tonight
8 P.M.
❀

Downtown Library

Do you know File Formats?

In this book we will mention EPS files and TIFF files and GIF files and JPEG files, and we have to assume that you know what they are, which programs create which sorts of file formats, what a native file format is, and how to work with each of them.

If you cannot answer these questions, read *From Design into Print: Preparing Graphics and Text for Print,* **by Sandee Cohen.**

1. What is a **native** file format?

2. What is a **raster** format?

3. What is a **vector** format?

4. What is an **EPS**?

5. What is a **TIFF**?

6. What is a **GIF** and when would you use one?

7. What is a **JPEG** file?

8. What is a **compression scheme** and when would you need to use one?

9. Which of the above-mentioned file formats are **compressed**?

10. Which file format, **EPS** or **TIFF,** prints better to a non-PostScript printer, like a color inkjet? Why?

11. In which file format is it best to **scan** photographic images for a print project?

12. Is the image below most likely a TIFF or an EPS?

13. Is the image below most likely a TIFF or an EPS?

What do you know about Fonts?

It used to be so different. A designer didn't have to know anything about "fonts" and very little about typography, but now most designers have to do everything. Knowing how to deal with your fonts technically is important so your work prints properly.

You don't **have** to know any of this stuff to be a great designer—but you have to know it if you produce your own work, **or** if you oversee the work of someone else and they don't know about font technology and **you** have to recognize the resulting problems.

If you cannot answer these questions and you use a Macintosh, read *Real World Mac OS X Fonts,* **by Sharon Zardetto Aker.**

Windows users (and Mac users), read *From Design into Print: Preparing Graphics and Text for Print,* **by Sandee Cohen.**

1. What is a **PostScript** font?

2. What is a **TrueType** font?

3. What are **OpenType** fonts and what is their advantage?

4. Which font files can be used on both Macs and PCs?

5. What is a **PostScript printer**? How can you tell if your printer is PostScript?

6. If you have a huge collection of fonts, you need a **font management utility.** Can you name three Mac font management utilities or two PC utilities?

7. How do you **install** new fonts if you are not using a font management utility?

8. In which situation do you want to avoid **TrueType** fonts?

Mac users only:

9. Each PostScript font has two parts. What are they?

10. Where must the two separate parts of a PostScript font be stored in relation to each other? (Knowing this answer will solve 98 percent of font problems.)

Do you plan to do Web Design?

The basic principles of design apply to all media. But each medium has its own peculiarities about how people work within it, how they use it, how they find what they need in it. The web is particularly different from any other medium. For instance, while watching a television commercial, a user does not need to figure out how to get from one part of the commercial to another—they just sit there and it happens. Most people know how to use a book and its table of contents and index to find what they need. But on a web site, it is the designer's job to make it easy for a visitor to **navigate** from one part of the site to the other, something we don't have to do in any other medium. Because we have covered this sort of material plus all the technical stuff about building web sites in another book, we won't be discussing it in this one, but we want you to know where to find that information.

1. Name at least five ways that **web design is different** from print design.

2. Does a web page look better with a horizontal **layout** or a vertical layout for the main design elements?

3. Are **graphics** on the web RGB or CMYK?

4. Which **file format** is most appropriate for photographs on the web?

5. Does a 300 **ppi** image look better than a 72 ppi image on the web?

6. Some **monitors** display photographs better than other monitors. What is it about a monitor that would make a photo look better or worse?

7. What **fonts** can you use safely in default text on a web page? What fonts can you use in your web graphics?

8. What is an **optimum file size** for a web page, including all the images?

9. What is **CSS** and why is it important?

10. What is **anti-aliasing** and how does it affect web graphics?

If you cannot answer these questions, read the *The Non-Designer's Web Book, third edition,* **by Robin Williams and John Tollett.**

11. Name six features of the web page below that give it an **amateur** look. Granted, few web pages really look this bad (well, probably more than we like to admit), but many pages have one or more of these features that scream, "I am visually illiterate!"

Keep an Idea File

No designer works in a vacuum. A standard tool in every designer's box is a **collection of books** that shows what other creative people around the world are doing. And you should keep an **idea file,** also called a swap file or a morgue, which is simply a file folder (or entire drawer) filled with ads that you have torn out of magazines, brochures, posters, bread wrappers, any item that grabbed your attention and you think was well designed. Put it in your idea file, ideally with a few notes about what exactly makes it so effective. When you start a new project, go through these books and ideas. This is not copying—it is a very traditional form of learning. When you see a good idea and apply the concept to your specific project, it adapts to your project, changes, and becomes your own.

This is a small part of our collection of design books. Every year new "annuals" are published, display cases of the best in typography, logos, general design, web design, and more. There are also many, many books teaching design and type, filled with great ideas and suggestions. When you're stuck for solutions, flip through them all and we guarantee you'll find an inspiration for a unique solution that you probably wouldn't have thought of without the benefit of the collective consciousness of designers around the world.

2. Taking Advantage of Clip Art

The term **clip art** refers to artwork created by professionals that you can buy inexpensively and use in your own projects. It comes in many forms—illustrations, photographs, as typefaces, full-color, black and white, and in different file formats—EPS, TIFF, GIF, JPEG, PostScript, or TrueType. Use clip art to juice up your work, create logos, inspire new ideas, or tie a theme together.

Occasionally you will find an image with restrictions that prevent you from using it as a copyrightable logo or trademark, even though other uses of the image may be practically unlimited (other than reselling it). Check with the vendor for any restrictions that may apply.

Typefaces in this chapter:
Galliard (ITC), which creates a little more sophisticated look than the Clearface in the first chapter.
Airstream (ITC), which ties in with the playful clip art look.
Officina Sans (ITC), a sans serif with a bit of character, but still a good, clean contrast to the other two typefaces.

15

The Variety!

There is an enormous variety of clip art available, as you can see even by the very limited selection on these pages! The different styles and different file formats you choose will depend on your project and the printing process you plan to use to produce the piece. (See *From Design into Print: Preparing Graphics and Text for Print,* if you are not sure about how to choose the correct format, resolution, and color model.)

You can, in effect, expand your clip art collection by altering the existing art in different ways. Use a piece of clip art and enlarge it beyond expectations. Apply an unusual filter effect on an otherwise ordinary selection. Combine different clip art styles to make one unique illustration. Just spend some time experimenting and you'll be surprised at how your imagination responds.

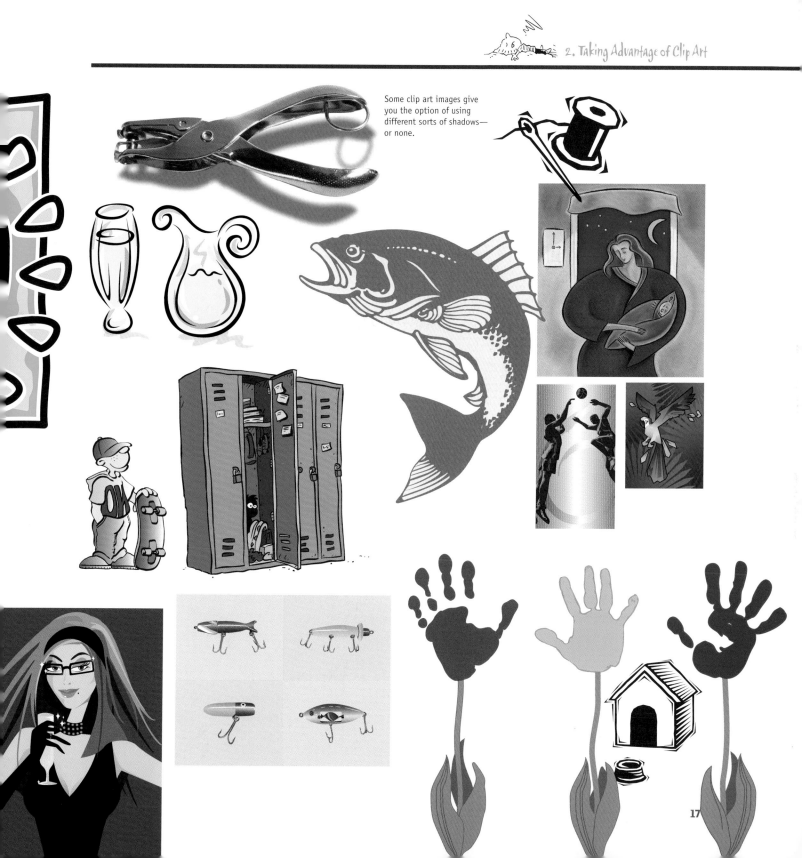

Some clip art images give you the option of using different sorts of shadows—or none.

Clip Art Fonts

Besides clip art in all its graphic file forms, there is also a large variety of picture fonts that can be used as clip art. The advantages of using a font as clip art is that you get anywhere from 30 to 200 or so pictures for the price of a typeface, the images are easily resized, they print clean and sharp to any printer these days, and you can change their color as easily as changing the color of any letter in your text without having to open any other application.

You can type a character into an illustration program such as Illustrator, FreeHand, or CorelDraw, change it to outlines, and colorize individual parts. Or you can outline and customize it directly on the page in InDesign. Or type the image into a program like Photoshop and make web graphics.

Art Three

Backyard Beasties

18

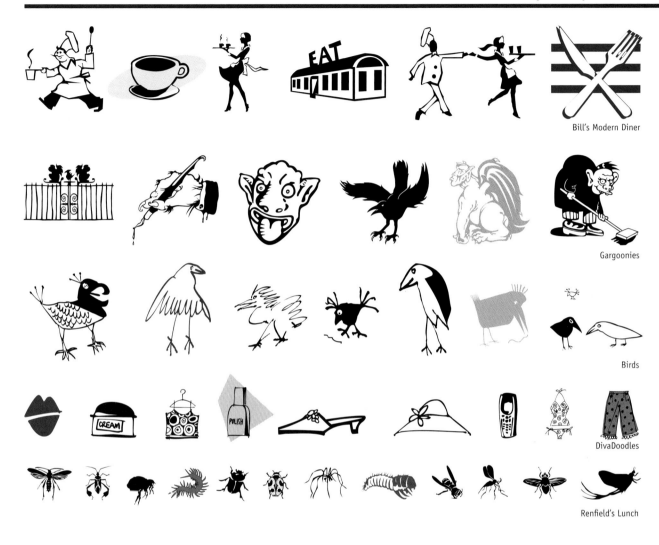

Bill's Modern Diner

Gargoonies

Birds

DivaDoodles

Renfield's Lunch

PLEASE come to the
Company Picnic!

Robin's Roost Bookstore
snuggle up with a book

Old Pecos Trail
Santa Fe
New Mexico
87505

505.555.5555
www.RobinsRoostBookstore.com

Fontoonies

Backgrounds, Borders, and More

Don't forget about the other graphic elements you can buy, such as backgrounds, borders, frames, and ornaments. Since they are so accessible and are relatively inexpensive, these objects are worth adding to your collection of graphic tools. Use them in unexpected places and in unexpected ways.

An incredible variety of textures is available: canvas, adobe, marble, mud, burlap, stone, dirt, velvet, silk, exotic papers . . . ad infinitum. Backgrounds can add richness and visual interest to a design or be an effective way to provide visual continuity to a series of pieces.

Everybody loved Mabel

Frames from Auto FX

font: Type Embellishments One

font: Type Embellishments Two

font: Golden Cockerel Initial Ornaments

There are thousands of images available to use as backgrounds. In your image editing software, fade the entire background back, or just a part of it, so you can overlay text or other images. Try them on brochures, posters, book covers, etc.

Women & Reading

An Illustrated History

Ima Reader, PhD.

Use a border on a flyer, invitation, recipe, poem, cover, announcement, or any other item you want to fancy up.

Take an ornament, enhance it in an image editing program like Photoshop, and use it as a dramatic visual element.

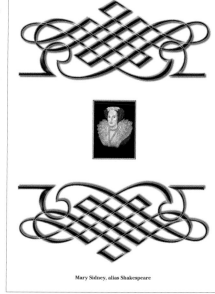

During Shakespeare's lifetime, Mary Sidney was famous and he was a nobody. Now he's famous and you've never heard of her. There's a reason for that and it's going to change the literary world.

Mary Sidney, alias Shakespeare

These borders are from Aridi Computer Graphics, the Olde World collection.

The graphic images inside the invitation are characters in the font called Fontoonies.

Please come to our wedding. Win a chance to drive the getaway car.

Creative Clip Art

There is such a huge variety of clip art that it is easy to use it "as is" and create something just wonderful. If you have the tools and know-how, you can open clip art in an appropriate application and alter it to suit your specific need and make it look even less "canned."

On these pages are examples of clip art used in typical design projects. Some images are straight out of the box and some have been manipulated.

DO YOU HAVE A PLAN FOR YOUR FUTURE?

Wants pawn term dare worsted ladle gull hoe lift wetter murder inner ladle cordage honor itch offer lodge, dock, florist. Disk ladle gull orphan worry Putty ladle rat cluck wetter ladle rat hut, an fur disk raisin pimple colder Ladle Rat Rotten Hut.

Wan moaning Ladle Rat Rotten Hut's murder colder inset. Ladle Rat Rotten Hut, heresy ladle basking winsome burden barter an shirker cockles.

FUTURE SHARE
FINANCIAL PLANNERS

Call 1-800-555-5555 for the FutureShare nearest you.

John altered the edges of this illustrative clip art and added the shadow.

Notice he brought the black box up into the clip art image; the box acts as a unifying element to tie together the various elements in this ad.

He pulled a color out of the illustration and applied it to the business name (the principle of repetition), while leaving all the other elements black. This does two things: it gives the color image more impact by not having to compete with other colorful elements, and it makes the business name pop out of the page.

The ad above uses clip art characters from a font. In the page-layout application, they were selected and their colors changed. To the left you see how strong the same ad is even in black and white.

Notice the logo also contains the clip art character.

The ad to the right uses clip art and some great type, along with the same logo as above.

There are so many wonderful images available—all it takes is a little imagination and a good font combination to make effective and award-winning pieces with clip art.

Watch your COMPOSITION

The composition of a photograph (or a layout) refers to how the elements of the image are arranged and manipulated to direct your attention through the image or design. This is done with the visual suggestion of the direction of lines and form, the emphasis created by lighting, color, contrast, and size.

A well-designed photo has been planned with an awareness of composition and with a conscious attempt to control a viewer's focus and attention, leading the eyes from one point to another in a particular order.

An effective composition can be subtle and unobtrusive or it can be a flashing, neon sledgehammer, depending on the style and tone you want to convey.

For some great tips and techniques on taking your own photos, go to the Kodak web site (www.Kodak.com), find the Consumer Photography section, and click the link "Taking Great Pictures." It's a wonderful resource.

The most common problem is the most fixable— take a good look through the viewfinder of the camera. Look for a stovepipe coming out of the top of someone's head, half-eaten food, wrinkles in clothes, odd shadows, unnecessary clutter, and anything that is not visually pertinent to the image. If you can't move the object, move the photographer.

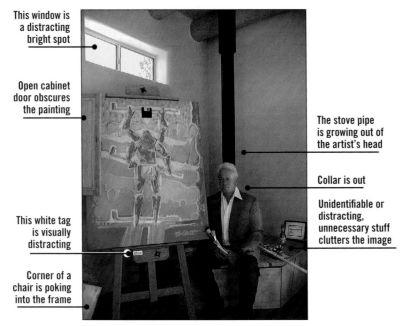

This window is a distracting bright spot

Open cabinet door obscures the painting

This white tag is visually distracting

Corner of a chair is poking into the frame

The stove pipe is growing out of the artist's head

Collar is out

Unidentifiable or distracting, unnecessary stuff clutters the image

Let's say you're taking a photo of some of the members of your bike club on their cross-country trip. This is a typically bad shot—there are telephone poles and wires, overflowing dumpsters, and other superfluous, distracting, and downright ugly stuff in the photo. Since you can't move the poles and the dumpsters, move yourself!

Can you tell who's who with their helmets on? No? Then let go of trying to identify each person and instead focus on another interesting aspect that will make a provocative image for the newsletter.

Don't always crop in tightly when taking the photo. If you leave a little extra space around the image, you have more options for layout design later. Professional photographers tend to compose the image beauti fully through the lens, but that means you might have fewer choices in how you use the photo later.

Take photos from different viewpoints. A simple change of origin can turn an average photo into an interesting one. (For this particular image of a dinner party, we ran an artistic filter on it because even though we liked the photo, it wasn't a technically great one because of the lighting conditions.)

Experiment with CREATIVE CROPPING

Just because a photographer hands you a photograph or you pay good money for a stock photo doesn't mean you have to use it exactly as is. Many photos benefit from judicious or creative cropping. Even a fabulous photograph might need cropping to make the advertisement or poster more exciting, create a focal point, or emphasize a concept.

*g*inely fodder beer gutter grade bag short-gum, Murder Beer gutt muddle-sash haunting flean Ladle Bore Beer gutter tawny ladle pestle, an oiler beers crypt upper stars, ware Guilty Looks worse line honor bet, sunder slip an snorting. Herring door beers, shay weakened, lipped otter door windrow, an dished aware harm jesters fascist shagged scrabble.
505.555.4519

realtor g

first night in a new home

Here we have a nice, predictable happy-couple photograph (above). It's nice, but we've seen its clone at least a hundred times. Since the ad focuses on the emotional experience of a new home, we cropped in to focus on the couple yet retain the moving boxes and takeout (and really lost nothing in the process). The ad copy reads right down into the couple, reinforcing the message that this is about a human experience. The busy stuff on the left side of the photo helps balance the ad copy in the upper right.

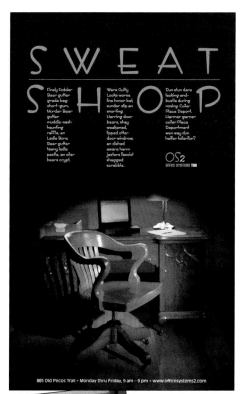

We applied a painterly effect to this photo, then cropped it into an elliptical shape to create a dramatic visual focus.

Photographs can have accidental details and ideas hidden in them. We often crop in tight on just one detail of a complex photo to get a stronger visual impact.

For this recruiting poster, we liked the rowing image, a symbol of teamwork and striving for excellence. But we've all seen the "teamwork" type of poster—we needed something unique. So we severely cropped the image and added an unexpected element, the badly off-course wake. We posterized the photograph for a more dramatic effect and added a headline in youth-culture jargon to further emphasize the point.

Check out the new age of
STOCK PHOTOGRAPHY

Digital layout and design has created an explosion of available images that is stunning in its diversity, not to mention the ease, convenience, and affordability of searching for and acquiring stock images.

If you've never heard of or used stock photos in the past, they are simply photographs, generally fairly generic sorts of scenes, shot by professionals, that are then sold to you and anyone else who wants to buy them. It is much less expensive and much faster to buy a stock photo than to hire your own photographer and models and have the shot made.

A huge variety of styles, themes, and subject matter is available. You can buy a single image, a single CD full of images, or a bundle of CDs with more photos than you'll ever be able to use.

Are you one of those who can remember ordering a stock photo, then waiting for days for it to arrive by mail, and then having to send it back when you were finished with it? If you don't remember that, consider yourself lucky and start using stock photos. A list of a few popular suppliers is on page 44.

Gather ideas from photos

You can also use stock photos as an idea resource. Browse through the image CDs you own, or go online and (for free) see what ideas and concepts you can relate to your own design projects. You'd be surprised how many ideas start appearing. A photograph may give you an idea that leads to a solution that doesn't even need a photo.

Check out the "Shuttleboard Mode" of Veer.com's lightbox where you can play with combinations of type and images.

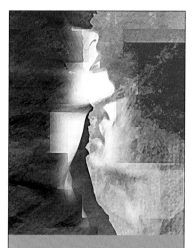

*So, at his bloody view,
her eyes are fled*

*Into the deep dark cabins
of her head.*

William Shakespeare
Venus and Adonis
lines 1037–38

*A new
play by
Ryan Nigel*

Some
day

*Scarlett Williams
Dakota Max*

New Globe
Productions
· · · ·

Jimmy lost
his innocence
today.

He watched TV.

Deadline
PRESSURE
?

Techno Jazz Experimental Quartet

Experiment with
BLACK AND WHITE

Black-and-white photographs can be even more provocative and attention-getting than color photographs when used unexpectedly, as in a four-color magazine or brochure. The stark contrast and visual impact of a black-and-white image in our full-color world can make a powerful and dramatic statement.

Black-and-white photos can set a tone or mood in your design. Because you must be brave to use a black-and-white photo in a full-color project, it can automatically make the piece look artsy and trendy.

You can't rely on color to carry the photo or fool people into thinking it's a great image; black-and-white photos (like movies) need to be more carefully crafted, relying more on composition, dramatic effect, and contrasts. It's rare that you can take just any standard stock photo, make it black and white, and let it go at that. Plan to spend a little more time composing, cropping, tweaking, and manipulating a black-and-white image.

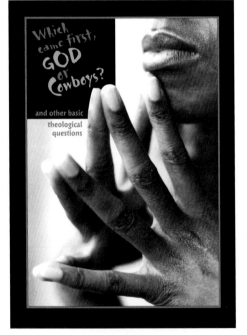

The contrast of the black-and-white photo with the colorful typography allows a visual contrast in this piece. The unexpected size of the image creates a strong visual impact.

"Black and white" doesn't necessarily mean black and white. That is, if you're using other colors in your job, try printing the "black-and-white" photo in another color. Try printing onto different paper colors, or onto white paper but with a subtle (or not so subtle) block of color behind the photo.

In your image editing program, apply a mezzotint filter (shown below, left) or add "noise" to the image (below, right) to give it a different texture.

Experiment with printing the black-and-white image in a color with an extra-large dot pattern. Notice the different effects you can achieve using dark or light ink colors, combined with different paper colors.

Try a dash of spot color on your black-and-white photo. The combination of strong, bright color on the stark photo can be very eye-catching.

Try a DUOTONE

You can make a black-and-white photograph appear richer in tonal value by printing it as a **duotone.** In this technique, the shadow tones print with a dark ink (usually black), and a lighter ink (another color) is used to print the mid-range and light values. Depending on the second color you choose, the effect can range from subtle to harsh.

A variation of this is to use a gray ink instead of a color ink for the mid-range and light values, which retains the basic look of black-and-white photography but the overall tonal values are much richer than in an ordinary halftone.

For two-color projects, a duotone is a great technique that adds beauty and richness. Even in a full-color project, you get the impact value of the black-and-white photograph, but with a more elegant look. Keep in mind, though, that the second color is typically a spot color, so creating a real duotone in a four-color project often involves paying the extra price for that spot color.

Tritones and quadtones are similar to duotones, but obviously use three or four inks instead of two—this means two or three *extra* colors printed as spot colors. If the job is four-color process already, paying for two or three spot colors is usually prohibitively expensive for all except the most wealthy client (but when it can happen, it's great).

(For specific details on exactly how to create duotones, tritones, and fake duotones, please see *From Design into Print: Preparing Graphics and Text for Print.*)

Another approach is to create a **fake duotone:** instead of making a halftone with two different values and printing the different values in different colors, create a solid color (or percentage of solid color) behind the image; the photo prints on top of the block of solid color, as shown below. This technique isn't as subtle as a real duotone and the range of tones isn't as rich, but it can give you another image style to work with.

To the right is a true duotone. Below, left, is a fake duotone using a background of a teal color in a value of 100 percent. Below, right, the background is 60 percent of the teal color.

Apply Creative
SPECIAL EFFECTS

The digital imaging tools in electronic graphic design encourage you to experiment with images and create effects that you could never imagine before you started clicking those buttons. In addition to the many special effects filters and capabilities built into the most popular image editing software packages, there are hundreds of third-party plug-in filters available that can turn ordinary images into amazing visuals. Experiment with them—learn to use your software!

For instance:

› Add colorful embellishments to ordinary photos.

› Change the color from ordinary to unusual or unrealistic.

› Make a photo partially color.

› Experiment with different compositing modes between layers.

› Invert the image.

› Saturate or desaturate the color.

Photoshop filters can add visual interest or even salvage a photo of inferior quality. We applied the "Cutout" filter to this image. The airbrush effect of soft color gradations in flat areas of color was achieved by over-sharpening the image using large "Amount" and "Radius" settings in the "Unsharp Mask" filter dialog.

This is the original photo.

Monotone(ish) photographs don't have to stay monotone. In Photoshop, you can add color using the "Curves" dialog box; experiment with manipulating the curves graph line.

A posterization filter adds impact when you want your image to have a graphic look rather than a photographic look.

This is the original photo.

Extreme closeups can be even more dramatic with unexpected color. Try using the "Hue/Saturation" sliders in Photoshop.

Natural media filters, such as this chalk effect, can create unique images and eye-catching textures.

Adjust the hue, saturation, and contrast of images by manipulating Photoshop's curves. You can create unlimited color variations that add pizzazz to your design.

*You can selectively control how much color appears and exactly where it appears using the saturation tools. Of course, a technique should be used to **enhance** your message, not merely to prove you can use Photoshop.*

On the image below, we painted colorful squiggles directly on top of the graphic. It makes a potentially boring and predictable icon a little juicier.

John transformed this photographic montage of office icons (a stock photo) into an illustrative painting.

An already great shot can be turned into an even stronger image (as long as it suits and enhances your project). John used a "Poster Edges" filter on this sunset and increased the color saturation.

He used the same filter on the photo of Robin's SwanMobile, below, to make it more graphic.

John opened this photo in Corel Painter, a "natural media" software package. He duplicated (cloned) the original image using a spatter brush.

Don't Forget
STOCK ILLUSTRATIONS

As with stock photography, the selection and variety of stock illustrations has grown tremendously with the advent of digital delivery. These illustrations, available in both full-color and grayscale (or you can just convert a full-color image to grayscale if necessary), come in many different styles covering a vast selection of themes, concepts, and subject matter. You can alter them to suit your needs, just as you can photographic images.

Like stock photos, you can browse through a CD or through samples online. Look for images to spark ideas for whatever project you're working on.

Where to buy
STOCK IMAGES

There are a number of vendors that sell stock images, both photographic and illustrative. Before you buy an image, be sure to check the licensing agreement; there are usually two kinds of agreements—"royalty-free," as well as "rights-protected."

Royalty-free images are quite a bargain. They're usually sold to you outright for a flat fee; you can use it however you choose and as many times as you want. Along with all this freedom comes the disadvantage of non-exclusivity: it's possible that the same image you're using could be bought by anyone else (including your competition) and used in the same way at the same time.

If it's important that you have more exclusive rights to a particular stock image, you can choose **rights-protected images.** These are not offered as royalty-free—you "rent" them for a specific use and sometimes for a specific length of time. To prevent any overlapping of usage and to give the appearance of exclusive use, the copyright owner (the stock image provider) keeps track of who is using which images, as well as how and where they're being used. The more exclusive your agreement, the higher the fee. The scope and exposure of your project can also affect the fee.

Most stock image providers can provide **single-image downloads** from their web site, or they can ship a CD directly to you. Royalty-free single download prices are very reasonable and are usually based on file size. Typically, a 600K, 5x7-inch, 72 dpi image file is very inexpensive (something like $25); a 10MB, 5x7-inch, 300 dpi image file is medium-priced; and a 28MB, 8x11-inch, 300 dpi image is more expensive (like $150 and up).

iStockPhoto has amazingly affordable images.

Veer
www.Veer.com

iStockPhoto
Very affordable images!
www.iStockPhoto.com

FotoSearch
Searches lots of sites at once.
www.FotoSearch.com

Shutterstock
www.Shutterstock.com

Comstock Images
www.Comstock.com

StockPhoto
www.StockPhoto.com

Getty Images, Inc.
creative.GettyImages.com

The Bettman Archive
is now owned by Bill Gates.
pro.Corbis.com

There are many others.
Go to the web and search for
"stock photo."

4. Understanding Design Challenges & Approaches

It's interesting how often design projects are thought of as design "problems." This is probably because we find ourselves searching for solutions to the "problem." The very phrase "design problem" can be intimidating if you haven't had a lot of experience as a designer. It can even be intimidating if you're an experienced designer—most of us would rather not work on a "problem." But a design "challenge" is much more fun than a problem.

As a designer, your challenge is to communicate visually, and not many jobs are more fun than that. So even if you're feeling a little inadequate, chances are you're much better equipped to accept this challenge than most people. After all, you're reading design books, aren't you?

In this chapter we used the following typefaces:
Large heads: **Firenze. 75 point**
Body copy: Bailey Sans, 9/12, which gives the text
   a contemporary, upscale look
Small heads: **Bailey Sans Bold, 10/12**

Limit Your Options

If you hire a thousand great designers to work independently on the same project, you'll get a thousand great and different solutions. There are many approaches and solutions to a design challenge; in fact, there are usually so many possible solutions that the first challenge is to **limit the options** to the solution. Otherwise you'll spend all your time deciding which approach to take and not enough time developing several good ideas.

Limiting factors

In any design project, there are external factors that help to narrow the design focus, such as the information and preferences gathered from client consultations, as well as the considerations of the target audience. These help to narrow your choices right away.

These restraints are not bad things—once you know what elements (or restrictions) are necessary, the rest of the design solution often falls into place more easily. Or at least it points you in a direction that helps to narrow the incredible number of solutions.

Four main restrictions

There are four main limitations in any job that help narrow your choices. Although you will naturally take these into consideration anyway, it helps to make a conscious note of them at the beginning of a project so you don't get side-tracked into an impossible choice. The four restrictions are:

> The reproduction process
> The client specifications
> The budget
> The deadline

Let's look at each of these factors and see how they affect your project.

Keep in mind that not one of these restrictions is an excuse for poor design. Many incredible projects have been created on cheap paper, a small budget, or in a hurry.

We do have a sign in our office, though, that states:

Good Fast Cheap
pick any two

1. Start at the end

The most limiting factor of any design job is the end process—how is the job going to be reproduced? For instance, if it's a newspaper ad or phone book ad, you need solid typefaces that will hold up well under the process and the paper, your color options will be limited (probably to black, if it's placed in a newspaper), your illustration or photographic options will be limited to those that will reproduce well with the lower linescreen value used in newspaper work, etc.

But if the ad is for a slick magazine, you have more typeface options, perhaps color options, and a wider range of possible illustrations or photographs because it's printed on smooth paper with higher resolution.

› In a magazine with glossy paper and high-quality printing, you have few physical limitations. You can use very fine type and high-resolution images with subtle gradations of tone.

In this layout, the high-quality printing process allowed us to use subtle colors in the headline and body copy without worrying that the type will fall apart. Even the fading of the type in the illustration should reproduce well on a high-end printing press.

› Newspapers and phone books are printed on absorbent paper and the images generally need a low linescreen value. So it's best to limit your typeface choices to those without fine details or thin lines, choose images that will not degrade in the printing process on cheap paper, and avoid using small type in gray because the linescreen dots will make it difficult to read. These limitations also apply to any other inexpensive reproduction process, such as copy machines and faxes.

For the newspaper version of this ad, we changed the subhead and body copy to black to avoid reproduction problems. We enlarged the illustration and eliminated the faded quotes since they might be unreadable when converted to a coarse newspaper halftone. Then we adjusted the layout to accommodate the changes.

2. Client specifications

As you begin a design project, the client will usually provide specific information about the project that will limit your options and influence the look and feel of what you're going to design. For instance, the client might demand you use an existing logo, the company color scheme, or certain product imagery that literally shows the product, as opposed to concept imagery that sets a mood or gets emotional attention.

Here's a typical project with a long list of client specifications.

> Description: 8.5 x 11, 2-fold, 2-color flyer for vacation studio rental

> Use: as a direct mail piece to travel agents' mailing lists and brochure racks.

> Main copy: emphasize village life-style and high-tech features.

> Bullet copy: itemize sites of local interest, casita features, rental rates.

> Graphic elements: map, interior and exterior photos, logo, logo of the co-opting partner.

> Also, the client wants a corresponding ad for tourism and visitor guide magazines.

A common technique with which to begin a project is to place all of the required elements in the layout without giving much thought to what the final design will be, as shown above. The challenge is then to make all the pieces of the puzzle fit in such a pleasing way that the whole message is easy to digest at a glance.

Once you have all the pieces together, you can start having fun. As you move things around, play with fonts, and experiment with color, ideas will come to you and you'll start seeing possible solutions that wouldn't appear if you were looking at a blank space.

Once all the elements were on the page, we decided the little studio image could be a charming focal element. Since the project was limited to two colors, we rendered the illustration in those colors (and whatever tints and shades we could create from them). The resulting image actually became more interesting than a black-and-white photograph.

As we experimented with placement and type, it became obvious that the headline would have a lot more contrast and thus eye appeal if we made a dark shape behind it; we decided to make that shape reminiscent of the sky and hills.

To emphasize the high-tech message, we added the oversized satellite dish to the drawing. By making the headline two different colors, we added impact to the "get away" message and yet, using a repetition of color between the dish and the type, tied in the concept of "keep in touch."

We chose fonts with casual, fun, yet clean characters. To visually organize the substantial copy (always a challenge), we used shapes of color that repeat the loose nature of the illustration as well as the background shape behind the headline.

The result is a piece that is visually more interesting, yet still organized and easy to read.

Get away but keep in touch

Our guest studio is the perfect place to relax, escape the city crowds, surf the Internet, watch satellite TV, and explore the Land of Enchantment. There's plenty of free parking and your own private entrance.

Two and one-half acres of rolling hills and arroyos make rabbits, quail, and hummingbirds your nearest neighbors. Enjoy the 16-mile Santa Fe-to-Lamy hiking/biking trail 100 yards away. If you need a quiet retreat with satellite television and Internet access, Agua Fria Casita will add charm, pleasure, and convenience to your next Santa Fe stay.

Agua Fria Casita

For reservations and
for more information
visit www.aguafriacasita.com
or call 1-888-555-9762

Adobe Charm & Internet Access

This corresponding magazine ad is okay—it's nice and clean, the typeface is pretty, and it says what it's supposed to say. But it looks a little sterile compared to the final brochure, and there's not enough visual contrast to pull a reader's eye into the piece.

To coordinate more closely with the brochure, we repeated the heavy, casual type-face and the loose shape behind the headline. To create a stronger focal point, we divided the headline into an eye-catching focus with a contrasting subhead.

3. What's the budget?

The budget constraints impose limitations that sometimes make it challenging to find design solutions.

Restrictions are not a bad thing—they often force us to be more creative. If you can't afford to hire a photographer or illustrator or even pay for stock photos, you have to be more creative with typography and perhaps clip art.

True, it's *easier* to design a full-page newspaper ad than a 2x5-inch ad because a full-page ad automatically gets a reader's attention, no matter what it says or how boring it looks. But it's fun to work with the limitations and turn the negatives into the positives. And it's often very satisfying, as well.

> The example on the left shows a client who has money to work with. Large, full-color, slick ad.

> The small guy needs to turn her business negatives into positives: smaller company, more personal, less expensive than the competitors, etc. A small budget does not mean a project can't be well designed, creative, and effective!

4. The deadline approaches

The deadline impacts your design choices, particularly regarding outside services, like special photography or the time it takes to reproduce the job—a one-color piece will have a faster turnaround than a two- or four-color piece. And the deadline limits your choices for illustration or detailed photo-editing work—you might have to work with what you have rather than spend two days creating a brilliant Photoshop montage.

If there's not time to shoot a photograph, use type, color, and shapes to tell your story. In the example above, a beautifully messy font says "plaster" better than most photographs. The primitive tile shapes are all that's needed to illustrate the craftsmanship of laying tile. An oversized ampersand (&) connects yet separates the two artists and becomes a playful visual element.

You may not have time to hire a professional photographer, but if you have a digital camera (even a cheap one), you can usually grab a shot that will work great, given a little creative edge. John took the image above on-site during a five-minute digital photo shoot. He then cropped it, posterized it in Photoshop, and used a vector auto-tracing program to give it more of a graphic, hard-edged look. Almost any marginal-quality photo can be salvaged by applying creative image-editing techniques, even in a hurry.

Choose a Look

We may talk about creating a design, but what we really want to do is **communicate**—communicate an idea, a feeling, or a message.

Communication is the real reason we're designing something at all. And it's impossible to design anything without communicating *something*. The challenge is to control *what* message is being communicated. And that's where design comes in—design is the visual choices you make to enhance the communication of a message. Your design can confuse and blur the message or it can make it memorable and clear.

Since each design project has its own unique message to convey, try to give that message its own unique personality by exploring different conceptual and visual approaches. The following is a variety of very broad conceptual directions to consider before actually starting to design. For any given design project, several of these options may provide viable solutions.

Look through each of these examples with a current project you are working on in mind; one of them might apply to your message. If so, many of your design decisions are already made.

In this chapter we could create other categories and subcategories, but the visual point is simply that there are many different ways to approach every project.

The following examples relate to design projects such as print ads and brochures where the objective is to deliver a specific message. Other projects, such as designing logos, letterheads, and business cards, concern themselves more with creating an appropriate and memorable corporate (or personal) image, and we discuss that in Chapters 6 and 7.

The generic look

This look is conservative, unimaginative, and boring, a design with no personality. It's probably the least attention-getting look you can design. Even a horribly ugly design would stand out more than this approach (but, of course, an ugly, noticeable design sends some other message that you'd rather not communicate!). Designs like this are unfortunately common because they're easy and fast, and they don't take any effort of thought or imagination.

Some designers confuse this style of design with a professional, conservative, classy look. Perhaps it was all those things the first million times we saw it. Now, however, this look has become the elevator music of graphic design, but without the passion.

Now that almost every computer in the world uses Helvetica as a default, the potential over-saturation of this look promises to make your message disappear further into the background than you ever thought possible. Designers who haven't bored themselves into a creative daze or a fear-of-failure stupor actually enjoy experimenting with typefaces that have more unique looks and that convey personality.

We've been named
Top Dog
at the
16th Annual
Top Dog Design
Competition.

Here at Ballyhoo Creative we're proud of our designers. But award-winning design doesn't mean much to a client unless it's followed closely by award-winning sales. If your design team isn't winning awards and growing profits for you, try throwing us a bone.

Ballyhoo Creative

1422 East Kent Drive, New Truchas, CA, (555) 438-5555

Why this piece looks generic:

› It has an unimaginatively centered alignment.

› It uses the Helvetica typeface which automatically makes it look dated (like 1970s).

› There is not much contrast.

› There is not much white space.

› There are typewriter apostrophes, a clear sign of an unprofessional designer.

› The copy is good, but the design does not support the message.

The corporate look

A corporate approach is exceptionally neat, organized, and predictable, giving an impression of trust and dependability. If you're not careful, this approach can look more like the generic, no-personality approach. But the corporate look is more creative than the generic look. It's more flexible—you can create all sorts of variations within the framework as long as the overall composition is neat, organized, and readable.

In the examples to the right, even with the slightly bizarre illustration, the ad appears to come from a company that doesn't get too wild or too far out of the mainstream.

What makes these pieces look corporate?

> Strong, clean lines
> No superfluous elements
> Typefaces are not unusual or weird (although it is certainly possible to get away with odd typefaces in corporate pieces!)

If we decide to be more casual and playful with the headline, the overall neat, organized alignment and conservative layout still makes the ad work as a message from a responsible, solid-citizen corporation.

The clients think the wacky dog illustration is fun. So much fun, in fact, that they say it is inappropriate for this particular corporation. The designer can feel lucky she gets to keep the wacky headline font.

The visual-wow look

With this approach, your main goal is to grab a reader's attention with a bold image, a stunning photo, or a captivating illustration style. While this approach is usually meant to be visually shocking, it can work in a variety of situations, from conservative, low-key messages to wild, anarchic youth-culture designs.

In the example top-right, the image of the dog is so bizarre and whimsical that you can't stop yourself from looking at the piece and you'll probably even read the ad copy. A simple piece of art used in a provocative way can be just as arresting as a photograph or a complex, technically amazing illustration.

It's always fun and often productive to keep exaggerating the focal point of the layout to see how far you can take it. In the top example, we thought the dog was a large visual element until we started experimenting with how extreme we could get. In the resulting example, lower-right, the contrast between the massive black dog and the white background is a visual magnet for a reader's eyes. If we went one step further and made the almost-abstract shape of the dog an unexpected color, such as puce or olive, we might take the visual-wow factor up another notch yet.

What gives these pieces their visual impact?

> ‣ Oversized, bold, simple graphic

> ‣ Strong contrasts—lots of black and white with small dashes of color

> ‣ An interesting headline typeface, one that is simple yet has a subtle "designer" quality.

The info-heavy look

This approach is useful for presenting a lot of detailed information and creating a formal, professional impression. You want to get someone's attention by showing how many features or advantages you have or by how expert you are. A simple, well-organized design makes it easy for the reader to scan a lot of information.

In the example to the right, you can instantly tell that it's a factual presentation of information, even though it uses a lighthearted, fun illustration. With this much copy in the ad, the reader gets the impression that the business must be serious about what they're saying so maybe you should read it (although some designers/copywriters take this thought to the extreme and present so much text that the chances of it being read become very slim).

When the copy is lengthy, use bold subheads so the reader can scan the main topics with a glance. Remember that a large portion of readers are not going to read this much text. The only chance you have of pulling any readers in is to create visually attractive and conceptually interesting headlines and subheads—their eyes will scan the heads and subheads, and if they're still interested, they'll read.

In this example, we turned the headline into a visual element and left white space around it to leave some breathing space on this text-heavy piece. The breathing space encourages a reader to dive in because it prevents an overwhelmingly textual appearance.

What makes this text-heavy piece look so clean and organized:

> Strong alignments of text, clean lines of columns.

> White space is gathered into organized areas instead of being interspersed between many different elements.

> Repetition of the black bars at top and bottom ties the information together into a neat package.

> Conservative combination of typefaces.

> Relatively small units of information grouped together; the reader reads one small chunk, then doesn't mind reading the next small chunk, and so on until the entire ad is actually read.

The omnibus look

The term "omnibus" refers to dealing with numerous items or objects at once. Omnibus designs are fun to create and to read—the image variety combined with short blurbs of text is irresistible to most readers.

With this approach you create a dazzling array of visuals using a variety of photographic and illustrative styles, each item with its own short blurb of text. This look works well for brochures and larger print ads where you have room to use a lot of images and still make the text large enough for easy reading. Because this is a casual, fun approach, the text can often be casual or humorous as well.

Be careful using this approach in a small ad because the images can lose their visual impact and the text might be too small to read comfortably.

What's going on in this omnibus ad?

> This design gets your attention, but it's not as strong as it could be. When visual elements are approximately equal, the reader doesn't know where to begin reading. **Something** has to be the boss. An omnibus ad is stronger if there is an emphasis, or focus, on one of the visual elements.

Above, the boxed headline is a strong element in this design and overall it's an interesting layout, but if we play with it and try exaggerating parts, it may get better.

Compare the example above with the two ads on the opposite page.

With a simple change . . .

> This design variation puts more emphasis on the "top dog" theme with the dog/star illustration (which is a piece of clip art). This illustration is now the largest element, and the dog is cute enough to get attention. But at this point we started wondering if we were being wimps—let's go ahead and put a *really* dominant image in the layout.

Let's strengthen it even more . . .

> Now the design has a much stronger impact with the huge, black dog that drags a reader's eyes into the piece. Once their eyes are on the page, they get pulled into seeing all of the surrounding colorful and interesting elements. Even though there is a lot of copy, it's broken up into short blurbs that tempt the reader to actually read them.

The typographic look

Don't think you have to use fancy graphic images in everything you design. Great type can be eye-catching and deliver an emphatic message with just a glance. The type might be stark or it might be an elaborate typographic treatment that becomes a piece of art in itself.

With the thousands of typefaces to choose from (or even with the measly few hundred on your computer), you have an inexhaustible supply of "looks" you can achieve, depending only on how creative you are.

Typographic design solutions are fun to work with and they're lifesavers when you have an unreasonable deadline or an extremely tight budget. Once you start experimenting with a typographic design, you usually end up with so many different ideas and versions that it's hard to narrow the choices to only one solution.

How about a fairly conservative yet strong look.

> A large, classic serif typeface with extremely tight letter and word spacing contrasts well with the small type flowing above and below the key words of the headline.

> A clean sans serif face for the body copy presents a no-nonsense approach that coordinates with the classic style of the headline.

Type can give the impression of a graphic.

> When you start playing with type, it's easy to create endless but similar variations of the same design. Be sure to completely change direction occasionally, trying different typefaces and various arrangements.

Depending on your market, you can get quite wild with type.

> "Lawless" typefaces can be used in just about any sort of piece, including the most conservative (depending on how and how much you use it). This piece uses both grungy and traditional faces together, with an emphasis on the grunge.

> Don't snub your nose at grungy type! Sometimes using just a wee bit on a page can give the impression that your company belongs in the twenty-first century.

The trendy look

What's trendy is always changing. An odd thing we've noticed as we've grown up in this design world is that before the digital age, trends used to last longer; then for a while there were a lot of changes as the technology allowed us more options. But now that we've been digital for these 20 years or so, design changes seem to be slowing down. Good, solid design that communicates clearly always rises to the top in any trend.

Trendy design at the moment might contain elements of complexity as decorative embellishments to make the space look rich and current or high-tech. Extreme simplicity of layout or imagery adds a bold, contemporary look to graphic communications. Irreverent typography, such as turning a type character backwards or upside down, makes a statement that you're not following yesterday's rules—graphically or otherwise.

Don't knock trendy. Everything in life has trends—cars, eyeglasses, clothes, hair styles, music, architecture, movies, even type. Picking up on a trend does not mean you are giving in to anything—it simply means you are alive in the world today, not clinging to yesterday. We know designers who still insist on using Helvetica, which makes a design look like a beehive hairdo.

These examples look trendy because of these features:

> Thin lines wandering through the layout in a playful way.
> Bold and simple graphic with unrealistic color.
> Unusual type treatment in the headline.
> Text that's out of alignment or crooked.
> Type sitting directly on or under a line.
> Non-essential elements on the page for that "random" look.

Ballyhoo Headquarters

21976 East Joshua Road	New Truchas	CA	95403	P 505 438 5555
www.ballyhoohdq.com	bones@ballyhoohdq.com			F 505 438 5556
where design is an art form and art forms are designed				**Suzy Forthly**

Type within boxes

> Beginning designers often put boxes around type; it seems to be something that feels safe, that keeps the type contained and prevents it from floating away. But beginning designers usually set 12-point Times or Helvetica in tightly fitting boxes and it looks amateurish, which it is.

The trick to setting type in a box is to use a great typeface, set it small (typically), and leave breathing room around the type. The boxes need to be a conscious design element, not just containers because you don't know what else to do.

Ballyhoo Headquarters

where the advertising past

meets the present

and moves forward

into the future

your future could depend on us

1422 East Kent Drive
New Truchas, California
505 438 5555

www.ballyhoohdq.com

Random elements

> The technique of using random elements speaks to a certain audience. Do the items look random to you? They are. Do they seem to have any relationship to the message? Not necessarily. Even if you're ambivalent about the efficiency of this technique, pieces like this are incredibly fun to create.

Look Around!

With each design approach the primary goal is simply to get the reader's attention. Exploring visually creative ways to reach that goal is where the design fun begins. As you explore various approaches to your next design project, always remain open to ideas and directions you haven't used before.

As we've mentioned before, one of the best ways to get the creative ideas flowing is to collect a library of design books that showcase award-winning projects that you can browse through when you're not sure in which direction to go. When you see examples that appeal to you, think about what it was that made you notice that design and how you can use that technique or a similar one to enhance your project.

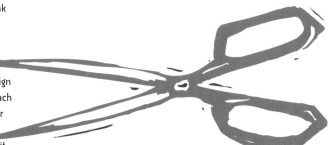

> **Designer Exercise:** Collect at least a dozen design pieces that you think are great. Make notes on each layout about the kinds of limitations the designer obviously had to work with—is it a low-budget job, something that could be done quickly, does it include and work with the corporate color scheme and logo, or was the designer given incredible creative freedom? If you see there are limitations, put into words how the designer creatively solved the problem within the limitations.

Let the ideas of other designers act as springboards for ideas of your own. Everyone needs to have the creative cobwebs shaken out occasionally.

5. Creating
Visual Impact

A graphic design almost always has three main goals: 1) Get attention; 2) create a memorable visual impression; and 3) communicate a message.

The best way to accomplish the first two goals is with **visual impact.** The design and layout of your project will determine if anyone stops long enough to see what you have to communicate. The greatest ad copy in the world will go unread if you aren't able to get the reader's attention. And the only way to do that is visually.

Basically it's all about **contrast—** contrast of size, color, direction, format, or a contrast of the expected versus the unexpected.

TYPEFACES IN THIS CHAPTER:
Goldenbook at 10/13 for body copy
    and at 90 point for large heads
A few callouts are in **Charlotte Sans Bold**

Size

Size—the size of type, graphics, the piece itself—is often overlooked when designing a piece that you want to have a strong impact. The trick to using size for visual impact is that it has to have a strong contrast. Making an element "sort of" bigger doesn't work— you gotta go all the way. And size doesn't always mean bigger. Often small works just as effectively, but it needs to be small IN CONTRAST to the rest of the piece.

Who has time to Cook?

Wail, pimple oil-wares wander doe wart udder pimple dum wampum toe doe. Debt's jest hormone nurture. Wan moaning, Guilty Looks dissipater murder, an win entity florist.
Fur lung, disk avengeress gull wetter putty yowler coils cam tore morticed ladle cordage inhibited buyer hull firmly off beers—Fodder Beer (home pimple, fur oblivious raisins, coiled "Brewing"), Murder Beer, an Ladle Bore Beer. Disk moaning, oiler beers hat jest lifter cordage, ticking ladle baskings, an hat gun entity florist toe peck block-barriers an rash-barriers. Guilty Looks ranker dough ball; bought, off curse, nor-bawdy worse hum, soda sully ladle gull.

Book-a-Cook
PERSONAL CHEF SERVICE

Disk moaning, oiler beers hat jest lifter cordage, ticking ladle baskings, an hat gun entity floris

In this example, size is the dominant impact in both the image and the headline. Setting part of the headline smaller enables us to make the other part really big.

By cropping the clip art image of the clock, we were able to make it larger as well, plus the cropped image is more interesting than just a flat picture of a clock on the page. Remember, when an image that we know well is cropped and going off the edge of a page, our minds fill in the rest of the shape. In design, this means we get to actually take advantage of "invisible space." That is, in this example, your mind "sees" the rest of the larger clock shape, even though it's not visible on the page. In fact, you probably unconsciously see the entire kitchen.

Even though this is a black-and-white piece, its impact is strong.

Obviously, the stark and simple illustration above is sized extra-large. It's simple, black-and-white, low budget, yet very eye-catching.

As we mentioned, "size" doesn't always mean "big." Let's say the example above is half of a newspaper page. Is there any way you could flip past that page without reading it? Hardly. That little tiny piece of copy has 100 percent readership. The secret is a **contrast** of size, either contrasting with other type or simply with the blank page.

A strong and surprising size can change a potentially dull, [almost] all-type piece into something striking. In this example, the conference initials become a large graphic element, bleeding off the edges. The same initials are sized even larger as a background element.

A blast of flat color in a bold and simple oversized illustration gets attention fast. The contrast of the size of the light bulb with the relatively small text makes the image seem even larger. And our minds fill in the rest of the shape that is outside the boundary of the ad, making the image seem even larger still.

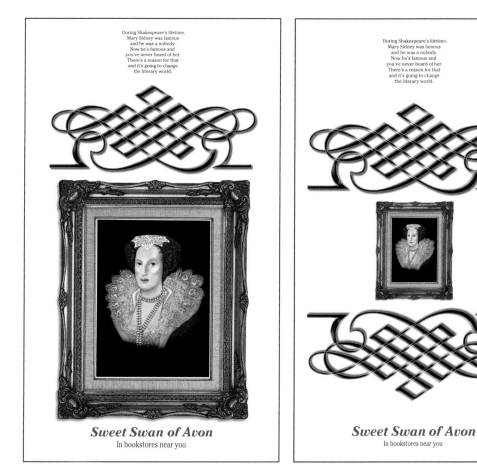

During Shakespeare's lifetime, Mary Sidney was famous and he was a nobody. Now he's famous and you've never heard of her. There's a reason for that and it's going to change the literary world.

Sweet Swan of Avon
In bookstores near you

During Shakespeare's lifetime, Mary Sidney was famous and he was a nobody. Now he's famous and you've never heard of her. There's a reason for that and it's going to change the literary world.

Sweet Swan of Avon
In bookstores near you

This project for a publisher uses a large, oversized ornament along with a large portrait to get attention and to set a 16th-century mood. The contrast in size between the body copy and the ornament, along with the ornament pointing toward the text, makes the body copy pop out of the white space even though it's small.

This variation uses a different arrangement of contrasts of size. Ornaments are usually small, delicate little things on a page. In these examples, the visual extravagance of the beautifully rendered ornaments is impossible to ignore. Remember, we're not just taking advantage of size as a visual impact, but the **contrast** of size.

The generous white space surrounding the smaller portrait would help this ad stand out on a page that holds other ads and editorial copy.

Black, oversized headline type dominates this layout, with a spash of contrasting color in the logo and illustration. Although we love the large type, its effect depends on contrast, and there's not much contrast between the headline size and the tag line size ("We deliver" is the tag line).

In this version, we reduced the type size of the tag line, which makes the headline type feel even larger and gives it more impact. We don't lose the tag line, though, because the contrast actually helps focus on it. Making the type size smaller also allowed us to make the panic-stricken customer a little larger.

Color

The impact of color is strongest when it's unexpected or extreme. Straight photographs of flower beds are lovely, but not necessarily exciting. Today we are all surrounded by so much color media of all sorts that we are able to visually accept just about anything you want to do with color in ways that would have been completely unacceptable years ago. So play with it, surprise yourself with it, push it.

And don't forget that color doesn't mean only "color"—color can be typographic black and white. Or it can be extremely minimal—it doesn't take much red (or any warm color) to make a statement.

The unexpected color in the portrait transforms this poster from a standard photographic approach to a visually arresting design.

The headline copy is blue, a cool color which recedes from our eyes. If we had made the headline a warm color like red, which comes forward, it would have created a conflict of focus between the headline and the portrait (not to mention a little confusing used with the word "blues," although sometimes you can use that sort of confusion to your advantage).

Color can be subtle and still get attention; in fact, it may get more attention than a regular full-color piece. In this example, the purple and black shapes create a visually interesting background that leads your eye vertically through the page and provides a powerful color contrast for the white type. If you can imagine a version with the photograph in full color, you can see that the focal point would be different, the eye flow would be different, and the entire page would not have as much impact, even though it would be more "colorful."

The jarring color combination in the stylized painting image set the tone in this brochure for a contemporary art gallery. The muted background colors add richness and a good contrast for the bright colors, emphasizing those colors rather than competing with them, and providing a visual respite so the garish green and orange don't overwhelm you. We could have picked up one of those colors or perhaps a tint or shade in the gallery name, but we chose not to interrupt the strong focal point of the image.

THUNDER ON THE LEFT PRESENTS

LIQUID NAILS

IN CONCERT

MARCH 17TH • 8 P.M. TO MIDNIGHT • FILMOOR WEST AUDITORIUM • SAN FRANCISCO

A four-color poster doesn't have to represent the full spectrum of colors. We colorized this black-and-white photograph in Photoshop to add subtle coloring, letting the headlines pop out in contrast.

Url's Internet Cafe WORLD HEADQUARTERS

John Tollett
The Big Boss

Santa Fe
New Mexico
87505

P 505 555 4321
F 505 555 1234
E url@UrlsInternetCafe.com

W www.UrlsInternetCafe.com

Warm colors are powerful and don't need much to make themselves known. The hard thing to do is convince your client to pay for the second color if it's only just a tiny bit; usually they say something like, "If I'm paying for a second color, then I want a lot of it!" You have to tell them that the tiny spash of second color is more powerful, has a stronger impact, looks more sophisticated, and it indicates that the carrier of the card has both good taste and money and is not a wimp.

The Unexpected

Very often in the design process, the first image or visual that comes to mind is the most expected, the most trite, the most pedestrian—which is exactly why it was the first thing that came to mind. So toss that idea and spend some time figuring out what evokes the intended message other than the ordinary, expected solution.

You might use an unexpected typeface, or a provocative piece of clip art instead of the expected photo. Or perhaps you apply an unusual technique to a common image, juice up the photograph, or play down a design feature that others might expect you to play up, which right there brings attention to a piece.

This doesn't mean a piece has to be bizarre or trange — it just means you want to move at least one step away from the mundane. The solution might still be formal and sedate, but it won't be dull.

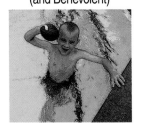

Eat, Drink, Splash, and Be Merry!
(and Benevolent)

Summer Pool Party Benefit
for the Leukemia and Lymphoma Society

Join us at Cliff and Julie's pool for BBQ, music, dancing, and lots of splashing and swimming to break the summer heat. Bring a swim suit. Your donation of $25 benefits the Leukemia and Lymphoma Society.
Date: August 15 **Time:** 10 a.m. until 10 p.m. **Address:** 4566 Powerhouse Road, Fremont, California

Sponsored by: **Book-a-Cook**
PERSONAL CHEF SERVICE
Visit www.bookacook.com or email chef@bookacook.com

This functional, tidy flyer uses some very predictable features: Helvetica/Arial font, centered layout, cute photo of boy in pool. So change each of the predictable pieces: Use a fun typeface. Experiment with other layouts besides centered. Trade the cute photo for a more unexpected image.

In this version of the same flyer, we changed the type-face to something more fun and playful. We switched the cute boy for a hilarious piece of clip art and set it on top of a colored blat (a blat is anything like that shape behind the clip art, which you can easily create in any page-layout application or illustration program). But the layout is still centered, and the three main elements are all similar sizes. Something needs to be the focal point; something needs to stand out more than everything else.

Since the illustration (which is actually made of two characters from the font Backyard Beasties, outlined and colored in Illustrator) is the most eye-catching element on the flyer, we made it the focal point. We organized the rest of the text in sizes appropriate to the hierarchy of information. We repeated the color and outline of the blat behind the body copy to visually hold all the detailed information together as one unit, and added another fun character from the same Backyard Beasties font as an illustration. And we uncentered the layout.

The unexpected element in this poster and ad is a conceptual one, referring to the Helvetica (also known as Arial) typeface as a language. This poster makes the point that many designers overuse Helvetica/Arial, forfeiting individuality and personality for the safe, predictable look that probably worked a thousand times before.

(It's not that Helvetica is ugly —it's a beautifully designed face. It's just that it was the most popular face in the world in the 1960s and was a way of life in the '70s. When anything is that trendy during a certain era, it forever influences everything it touches; it's extremely difficult to use Helvetica and not project a '70s look. Is that what you want? Let go and move on.)

Instead of the first images that comes to mind, a woman or a piece of art, we chose to combine a high-tech fractal to represent complexity and imagination within the silhouette of a female. Fractals are infinite; the closer you look, the more you see. Even if a reader doesn't understand fractals and what they import, they'll get the impression of complexity and creativity.

The first version of this poster design started with the basic elements on the page. We then created a basic, overused design format of centered alignment, large bold headline, and large image.

This design is clean and simple, but also boring because we've seen it millions of times. Our mission is to make the subject look richer, more complex, and more interesting.

For the next version, we reduced the size of the headline and changed the font to a casual script that's more compatible with the playful headline. A dark, neutral-colored background with elegant, drop-shadow ellipse shapes adds a feeling of elegance and sophistication.

We flipped the swan image horizontally, softened the edges, and added a dark glow around the edges. We applied a Photoshop filter (poster edges) to create a strong graphic look.

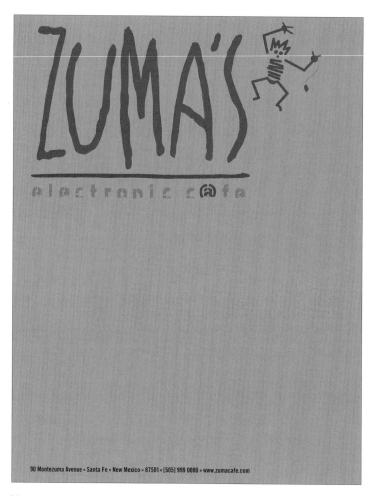

This ad, placed in an opera souvenir program, has several unexpected elements. It includes an unusual view of the Eiffel Tower, which becomes the letter "i" in "Paris." It uses a distinctive typeface, vibrant colors, and plenty of open space. The tag line flows like the winding river, and the cropped oval opens up the ad space because our minds fill in the rest of the shape.

You might expect a logo and stationery for an Internet cafe to look high-tech and trendy. But in this town (Santa Fe) where the ancient meets the modern everyday, the logo was given a petroglyph look and printed on stone-colored paper. The typefaces are a combination of grungy faces that represent the anarchy of the times we live in, yet the warmth of the old-fashioned care you get in the cafe. Also, you don't see many letterheads with logos this large—that's one reason we made it this large.

In this ad campaign for a private school, the viewer **expects** the child to write something like "6 x 48 =" or "I will not throw spitwads."

As the ad campaign continues with these unexpected ideas, the viewers learn to look forward to the new and surprising images that change on the blackboard, while the child remains the same.

Visual Puns

Visual puns are attention-getting, entertaining, and fun to see. They're even more fun to create. When you combine two or more thoughts into one image, the image becomes more compelling and memorable.

You might combine and juxtapose two seemingly unrelated elements, such as a gangster and a pencil, or you might put together strongly related elements such as the WORD "feather" and the IMAGE of a feather.

The pun, obviously, is in both words of the name, illustrated in the single visual image. Sometimes when creating a visual pun, the name comes first and then the image, or sometimes an image will inspire the name.

This logo went through a number of variations, as is typical in the design process — variations on the swashes, the emphasis and weight of the letter "f," the degree of slant, and other detailed features.

An image doesn't have to be elegantly rendered to be effective. In fact, a simple or crude image may have a certain charm not found in a more sophisticated rendering.

Some word combinations practically illustrate themselves. This logo for a band is a literal visual interpretation of the words—sometimes the most obvious solution is a good solution. In this case, the rendering of the idea is done in such a simple, bold, graphic style that even such an obvious solution is appealing.

To illustrate a common sort of identity deception, we show this despicable rat (Url) casting his alter-ego shadow.

An ad for winetasting classes uses this drawing, whimsically illustrating one of the attributes to notice in a glass of wine.

Don't be a wimp

Many projects need to be fairly conventional because of their markets, but it might surprise you how often you can get away with doing something off the wall. Try unusual typefaces, odd paper sizes, or weird graphics. For a particular project, write down all of the expected or usual solutions, such as typeface choices, images, paper size, paper color, ink color, etc. Then decide which of those features needs to be fairly conventional and which ones you can play with. On the features you can play with, don't hold back!

You are
warmly invited
to meet
my new
husband.

Friday
October 9
10 p.m.

Are you working on an invitation? Was your first thought to design it onto an 8.5 x 1-inch piece of paper, folded into halves or quarters? Why not try a tall, skinny look—divide the 8.5-inch width into thirds. You'll not only have an unusual invitation, but you can print three for the price of one.

mary sidney herbert

poetry reading
and
book signing.

monday » 3 p.m.

garcia street bookstore

505.123.4567

You don't have to make things extra-large to prove you're not a wimp —it takes even more courage to make things very small. The beauty and the effect of this ad lie in the fact that the small size is unexpected and creates a strong contrast. Our eyes cannot resist contrast. In a crowded newspaper, this ad would get 100 percent readership —it's not possible to open a page and ignore the surprisingly small type surrounded by lots of white space.

Are you working on a flyer? Instead of the standard vertical format, how about a horizontal one? Or try the horizontal cut in half, as shown below. Notice in the examples above and below, parts of the graphic and type are missing, but your eye "sees" the missing parts. Thus you get more visual impact in less physical space. Plus, the surprise of seeing type cut in half draws attention to itself.

Your attendance is requested.
Pinocchio Room · 3 pm · Friday · October 9
Be there or be fired.
sales meeting

Look Around!

Different design pieces appeal for different reasons, but in well-designed projects you will almost always find a strong form of visual impact that drew your eyes to that particular design. The more often you take a moment to NAME the visual impact, to put into words exactly what attracted your eyes, the more easily you will find yourself coming up with irresistible solutions.

Browse through your collection of design award books. Even if you've looked at the books dozens of times, you may notice something new in light of your current design project. You're not really looking for the exact solution to your problem, but for something to get your imagination fired up, perhaps going in a different direction than you originally planned. Or you may just need some inspiration or ideas for different illustration, typography, photography, or layout styles. Your final solution may not look anything like the example that inspired you, but it may be what was needed to get out of a creative rut.

> **Designer Exercise:** Collect at least a dozen design pieces that have strong visual impacts. Put into words exactly what the impact is of each piece and how the designer achieved it. If the impact is the result of a phenomenal photograph or piece of artwork, what did the designer do with that photo or art that strengthened the design?

PROJECTS

There is no single voice
capable of expressing every idea;
romance is still necessary;
ornament is necessary;
and simplification is not better
than complexity.

Milton Glaser

6. Logos

Hundreds of logos fight for attention with hundreds of other logos every day. If your logo design is going to have a chance of being noticed, it needs to have a unique personality that people will not only notice, but *remember.* In this chapter we'll look at some common techniques and themes of logo design that never get old because they are capable of unlimited variations and interpretations.

A designer whose portfolio has lots of logos in it has a great advantage because it says a lot of things about a designer: it says you know how to think visually and conceptually, and that you can take a complex communications challenge and condense it into its simplest and most effective form.

In all the chapters in this section
we used the following typefaces:
Large heads: **ITC Bailey Sans Bold, 60/60**
Body copy: Centaur MT, 10.5/11.8
Small heads: **Bailey Sans Bold, 10.5/11.8**

Designing a logo

Using creative typography along with simple visual/conceptual correlations between images and type is the key to solving most logo design challenges.

Experiment, experiment, experiment! You're using a computer, not rubbing down press-type or hand-tracing letters from a book of type samples, so play with all the possible combinations of faces. Not happy with your fonts, want to experiment further but you can't buy every font you want? You can see what your logo will look like in any of thousands of typefaces from a variety of different vendors: go to Veer.com, go to the "Type" section, then find the link to "Flont." You can choose a face, choose a type size, type your company name, and see it rendered in any font of your choice.

This logo is too busy—there are too many elements in this small space, too many gradations of tone that won't hold up well in many situations, and the typeface is difficult to read. Simplify for clarity, strength, and usability.

Often when designing logos, we go through versions like this (too complex) and then start revising it, reducing it to the simplest interpretation of the desired theme.

*The same logo is still fairly complex, but each of the elements will render easily in a variety of situations. Instead of setting **all** the type in the difficult face, we limited it to just the larger words and chose a contrasting, more legible face to work with it. We eliminated several of the extraneous elements. We managed to keep the client happy by adding a few details, like the dots and the tag line, but kept ourselves happy by making the details clean and simple. Most importantly, we concentrated on what would create the most effective **contrast**.*

Different files for different uses

For many logos, you will need to create several different files to be used for different purposes.

For instance, you might have a subtle drop shadow in a logo that works great when you use it in a slick, high-quality magazine. You might have a version of your logo in color for full-color brochures, and a low-res JPG or GIF version for the web. You need a version in black-and-white without the subtle drop shadow for newspaper ads, flyers that will be reproduced on copy machines, and your fax cover sheet.

Don't get attached to a particular design until you make sure it will translate well into all the different media it will be used in.

This is the full-color logo with subtle drop shadows that can be used in high-quality color printing, preferably on glossy stock.

This is the same logo in black-and-white, still with the subtle drop shadows because this version is for high-quality printing.

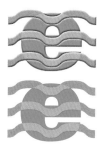

Here are two files of the same logo for an email service. The top one can be used where the printing and paper are high-quality, and a GIF version can be made from this for the web. The bottom one is useful for lower-quality printed pieces.

This version is the low-res GIF file to be used on the web. It doesn't look good in print, but looks great on the screen.

This black-and-white version is designed to hold up well in a newspaper, copy machine, or even a fax machine because there are no soft shadows that tend to get lumpy under poor printing conditions, and the contrast is stronger.

All type logos

Many logos are nothing more than type. But just because a logo is all type doesn't mean it didn't take creativity and skill to put it together. An all-type logo, used with a classic face, often creates a corporate look, a solid, dependable, no-nonsense sort of company. Think of the logotypes for IBM, Apple, or Pond's.

If you use nothing but characters, you had better be sure you're using excellent typography; check your letterspacing, linespacing, word spacing, the placement of hyphens or dashes, true apostrophes, etc.

ChromaTech   Helvetica/Arial

ChromaTimes   Times/Times New Roman

CHROMATECH   Avant Garde/Century Gothic

CHROMA*tech*   Palatino/Book Antiqua

If you plan to use all text as your logo, be very conscious of your type choice (duh). As a general rule, don't use any font that is built into your computer (like the ones shown above). Buy a new one.

Be especially wary of Helvetica (Arial is also Helvetica, it's just called another name). Helvetica was the most popular typeface in the world in the 1960s and '70s, so anything you create with it automatically has a '60s/'70s look. Do you want the same visual identity as thousands of other companies and organizations who still have their Helvetica logos held over from the '70s?

While we're on the font soapbox, please avoid Sand, Mistral, and Hobo for the next fifty years.

You can see what an incredible variety there is within the limitations of using one main typeface in the logo.

Combine typefaces

Very often in an all-type logo, you'll want to use two different typefaces. Sometimes you'll use two faces in the name of the company, or you might use a typeface in the large company name that is unsuitable for the small type. For instance, say you use a face with very thin lines in the company name, but you need to put the word "international," "incorporated," "corporation," or perhaps even a tag line like "We do it for you," in very small type. The thin lines that print clearly in the company name will completely fall apart in the small type, so you need a different typeface that will hold up in small sizes.

This is the key to using two (or more) different typefaces: **contrast.** You cannot use two fonts that have anything in common—if they are not members of the same family (like the very thin weight combined with the very heavy weight of the same font), then you must choose faces that are very different.

If you combine two faces and can tell they're not working well together but can't put your finger on it, look for the features that are *similar* between the two fonts—it is the *similarities* that are causing the conflict.

If this concept interests or confuses you, read the second half of *The Non-Designer's Design Book,* which focuses on the specific challenge of combining typefaces.

ChromaTech

This combination uses two members of the same typeface (Clearface); one is black italic and the other is bold italic. There is a bit of contrast between the two words, but not enough to be effective.

ChromaTech

This combination uses two different sans serifs (Frutiger and Avant Garde). They are slightly different, but have the same size, weight, and structure (monoweight strokes); these **similarities** create a conflict instead of a contrast.

CHROMATECH

This combination uses two different serifs (Garamond and Cresci). They are somewhat different, but both faces have serifs, a moderate thick/thin weight shift in the strokes, and both parts of this word are in all caps in the same size; these **similarities** create a conflict instead of a contrast.

ChromaTech

This combination uses two different scripts (Bickham Script and Redonda Fancy). They are somewhat different, but both faces have a thick/thin weight shift, curly shapes, hand-scripted forms, and they're about the same size; these **similarities** create a conflict.

This combination uses two different weights of the same sans serif typeface (Frutiger). Although they are from the same family, the difference in weight (thickness of the strokes) is so strong it creates a great contrast. If we combined the medium weight with the heavy weight, the contrast would not be so effective.

This combination is also two members of the same family (Clearface). The contrast comes from differences in weight (thickness), structure (expanded vs. condensed), and form (italic vs. roman), with a little contrast of color thrown in.

ChromaTECH

i n c o r p o r a t e d

This combination uses a modern face (Quirinus) and a sans serif (Frutiger). The contrast is in form (caps vs. lowercase), size (the caps are the size of the x-height), weight, and structure (serious thick/thin vs. monoweight strokes, plus serif vs. sans serif). The choice of color contrast is deliberate: cool colors recede. If we had chosen a warm color, like red, for the word "TECH," the warm color would have come forward, become more important, and there would be a conflict between it and the larger word (Chroma). The small type for "incorporated" is Frutiger.

Obviously, we've got a script (Bickham) combined with a sans serif (Impact). To intensify the contrast, we made sure to choose a heavy, rather vertical sans serif, and used the special, fancy initial cap that comes with Bickham.

The words "Kitt," "Katt," and "CAFE" are the same typeface, but KittKatt is Bodega Sans Black and CAFE is Bodega Sans Light. The contrast of weight and size is emphasized by a contrast of color. The ampersand (&), Redonda Fancy, uses a contrast of structure, color, and weight.

The modern font (Onyx), with its vertical, condensed serif characters contrasts strongly with the horizontal, cursive face (Carpenter). The contrast is emphasized with color.

SA&T

SCHOOL OF ART & TECHNOLOGY

The letters of SA&T are directly from the font Blue Island. The only logical choice of a contrasting typeface would be a sans serif—just about any other category of type (oldstyle, modern, slab serif, script, or another decorative face) would almost certainly have conflicting features.

This combination uses a tall, decorative, yet formal sans serif (Serengetti) in all caps vs. a playful, handlettered, childlike face in lowercase. In this logo, we also used a contrast of direction, size, and, of course, a contrast of color.

Tweak a letterform

Often logos involve tweaking a letterform out of the ordinary. This can be a very simple addition or subtraction to a character, or it might involve an illustrative technique.

Having letterforms interact with each other, as many of these do, adds visual interest and makes a typographic design more unique.

CHROMÆTECH INC.

This is simply an all-type logo with a red dot replacing the bar in the letter "A," which not only adds more visual interest to the logo, but provides a color spot that reinforces the word "chroma."

goldfeather

Once we saw this business name set in lowercase italic, it was an easy creative jump to see the letter "f" in the shape of a feather.

ADC

This logo for the Lamy Ad Club uses a strong combination of typefaces with a simple reverse of the overlapping stroke.

Robin   Robin
Robin   Robin

Truchas Art&Design

We pulled out the tail of the ampersand (&) to give this logo a more unique look and provide a subtle visual emphasis to the concept of "art" in the logo.

In each of these examples we simply substituted a small image of some sort for a character. The small images might be from picture fonts, clip art, original art, or just drawn shapes.

In the Integrated Marketing logo, designer Landon Dowlen customized the letters of the company.

Add elements

Many logos have symbols attached to the type. If you have lots of money and can afford to expose your logo excessively, the symbol can eventually stand alone, like the Nike swoosh, the Merrill-Lynch bull, or the Apple apple, and everyone knows who it refers to. But it takes millions of dollars and several years to do that—most symbols will stay with their logotypes rather than stand alone.

There is an entire study in symbology—all we are going to say here is that logo symbols are typically simple in form, with clean lines and shapes that will hold up well in a variety of media. If you look through design annuals and logo books, you'll notice that the symbols are often arbitrary shapes that have nothing to do with the logotype—they are simply marks (often common, everyday marks) that combine with a particular typeface and name of a company to create **a unique combination.** This *combination* of symbol, typeface, and name is the key—there are probably hundreds of logos that use a circle as a symbol in some way, but not in the unique way that *you* use it.

Ideally, you'd like the symbol to look like it belongs with the logotype. Often you'll see the two pieces set so far apart from each other that the connection is fairly obscure. Remember the rule of proximity—the space between elements creates a relationship; if the elements are close, they have a relationship; if they're far away from each other, they don't.

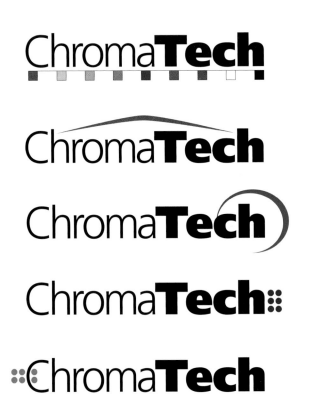

These imaginary logos each use a mark in addition to the company name. You can see that a mark can be very identifying, yet very simple.

logo by
Landon Dowlen

winery logo
by Landon Dowlen

Add clip art

There is so much great clip art available, including the dozens of images you get in one picture font. Not only is clip art great for using in logos, but just skimming through collections of it can give you great new ideas.

We repeated this little clip art of the lightbulb to represent both concepts of "idea" and "swarm." The font is naturally playful and unpredictable, but the entire logo is still a bit too static for a "swarm."

We bounced the type around to add energy to the letterforms.

In the process of adding more energy and visual interest, we created the unexpected element of a stray lightbulb that breaks away from the swarm.

TREVOR CLIFTON

computer geek to the rescue!

Emilie Brooke

writer

To customize the names, each of these logos uses an inexpensive piece of clip art or a character from a picture font.

Communication Consultants

TYLER MARSHALL *incorporated*

satellite communications experts

Postcard Machine **INFOMERCIAL.TV**

logo by Landon Dowlen   logo by Landon Dowlen

Prairie Rachel

star for hire

R&R Termite Control

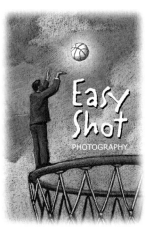

Easy Shot PHOTOGRAPHY

the **Soup Kitchen**

fine dining • fine wine

Don't forget the illustrative sort of clip art as a design option. Just remember that the logo should also work in black-and-white, so experiment with making the different files you need for various media before you finalize one solution.

Add illustrations

If you are a clever illustrator, like John, or if you can afford to hire an illustrator to help complete the logo, then you can truly customize your ideas in very unique ways. But don't let the lack of a professional illustrator stop you—a primitive illustration can have as much (or more) charm than a polished, professional one. In fact, often illustrators strive for that "unpolished" look.

There are a wide range of illustrations that work in logos. Just remember to keep it simple, and remember that any illustration must also render well in black-and-white.

This is a simple illustration, not much more complex than any of the elements we added to the variety of logos earlier in this chapter.

Tobacco Addicts Anonymous

This is also a simple illustration, using more creativity than high-end illustrative skill. Even if you're not technically an illustrator, it's amazing what you can do with an illustration program—push yourself.

Another simple illustration that takes more creative thinking than illustrative skills.

MetaNeo Gallery

This logo uses an illustration as the main element, since the image represents the gallery's focus so well.

logos above, above-right, and
below by Landon Dowlen

Each of these clever logos uses a custom illustration. Although this can be lots of fun, remember that every logo must still be able to be read and used in black-and-white, so make sure any illustration is flexible enough for all media before you commit to it.

Thunder on the Left

Thunder on the Left is a video production company. (When you hear thunder on the left, it means the gods have an important message for you.)

Handlettering is a form of illustration that works wonders in logos, but for most pieces it requires a experienced and skill to be truly successful. A logo represents your entire business; it's worth it to hire an excellent letterer if you want that look. This logo was designed by Brian Forsta of AgilityGraphics.com.

Having said that, go ahead and experiment with writing the company name dozens of times with different writing tools; chances are you'll find the beginnings of an interesting and unique logo. Some of the most wonderful handlettered pieces have been very "unsophisticated" letterforms taken from scrawls on walls, napkins, etc.

Look around

Logos are everywhere, literally everywhere. We guarantee you cannot open your eyes in any room and not see a number of different logos. The more you are conscious of them, the better you will design them.

Designer Exercise: Collect logos. Cut them out of the newspaper, phone book, brochures, bread wrappers, labels, boxes, print them from web pages, etc. Collect good ones and bad ones. Write the product or service on the back.

Separate the logos that have a corporate look. Even though you might not be able to define exactly what creates a corporate look, you probably know it when you see it. Once you have them assembled in front of you, put into words what they all have in common that makes them look corporate. Is it the style of logo (often all text)? Is it the size of type? The lack of an illustration? A fairly conservative symbol?

Separate the logos that look professional but high-tech trendy, the dot.com sort of logos. What exactly is it that helps you recogize this sort of company? What do the logos have in common? What is it that gives you that trendy yet professional sort of look? Is it a different style of typeface than a more corporate logo uses? Does it have energy built into it, and how does it manage to do that? Do any of the logos in this category use Helvetica/Arial, Times, or Palatino/Book Antiqua?

Separate the logos you consider to be not-so-good. Exactly what is it that makes them not-so-good? Is it the typeface or the combination of faces, the letterspacing, the size, the symbol, the relationship between the symbol and the type, the rendering of any image or handlettering, is it too busy or hard to read? The more you can state in words what makes a logo *not* work, the less likely you will build any of those features into your own creations.

Find the web sites that use some of the logos you've collected. Is the web logo different on the screen than it is in print? If you found a full-color logo on a package, see if you can find it in black-and-white, like in the phone book. How is it different? What did the designer do (if anything) to make it work both in full-color and in black-and-white?

Keep a file folder stuffed with logos, and buy books that showcase award-winning logos. Look through them before starting to design your own!

7. **Business**

cards, letterhead, and envelopes

Dear Sir,

Thank you

the inqui

response

ppertie

eat val

en hous

One of the first things any business needs is a business card, and next is letterhead and matching envelopes. It's best to design all of these pieces at the same time because you want them to be a cohesive package. If you design the business card first and plan to design the letterhead next month, you run the risk that the business card layout won't translate well to the letterhead. Even if you can't afford to have all the pieces printed at the same time, at least design them at the same time.

Business cards

A standard-sized business card is 3½ x 2 inches. Resist the temptation to make the card a larger, odd size—it won't fit in wallets or in many business card holders. When someone does put a large card in a wallet, the edges get all crumpled and the card looks shabby, which unconsciously reflects the image of the company whose name is on the card. Instead of trying to be creative in the size of the card, save your creativity for another area of its design.

If you *need* a larger card, experiment with a size that folds into the standard 3½ x 2; it might fold over the top, or the side might fold in part-way, or both sides might open out. You can be creative as long as your creativity doesn't encourage someone to throw away the card.

DOGGY'S BEST FRIEND
Boarding Kennels
Safe and Clean

123 South Frontage Road
Santa Fe, NM 87505

Ph. (505) 555-5555
FAX (505) 555-5550
www.doggysbestfriend.com

ACCURATE BUSINESS SERVICES, INC.
Business Brokerage, Appraisal, and Consulting

Harold P. Hocker
Licensed Broker and Appraiser

P.O. Box 1234
Santa Rosa, New Mexico
87555

Telephone 555-555-6543
Facsimile 555-555-5432
Toll Free 800-555-6543

These examples are typical of the kind of design you might find at a copy shop. Repeat these mantras:

It is okay to have empty corners.
*It is okay **not** to center the layout.*
*It is okay **not** to use all caps.*
It is okay to use a typeface other than Helvetica (Arial) or Times.
It is okay to use type smaller than 12 point.

It is okay to use one large graphic image instead of two small ones stuck in the corners.

With thousands of typefaces at your fingertips, there's no excuse to use a boring one. In the examples above, all we did was change the typefaces, set most of it in caps/lowercase, and provide *one* alignment (instead of flush right, flush left, and centered on one page). In the dog kennel example, instead of two little graphics stuck in the corners, we used one and made it a focal point.

Even though the bad example (opposite page) used a centered alignment and all caps and we discouraged that, the problem is not really with the centered alignment and all caps—the problem is with how those features are used. As you can see above, all caps and centered can make a beautiful arrangement. What's the difference? Why do the examples above look elegant and the examples on the opposite page look dorky?

› The first dorky example isn't really centered—only part of it is. The combination of centered, flush left, and flush right all in the space of a little card creates a mess; there's a lack of cohesion and unity. In each of the examples above, there is one line running down the center of every element.

› A centered alignment needs nice type and a pleasant amount of white space to be acceptable. When a piece is centered and all jammed together in a deadly dull face, it inevitably looks unprofessional.

› The size of type (in relation to the piece) can make all caps acceptable or not. Business-card text can be small. Setting type all caps in 12 point is redundant—either make it a focal point with larger type and a stronger face, or make it a subsidiary element.

The secret is to be conscious: If you can put into words why you choose all caps, go ahead. You might say, "I need clean, rectangular shapes in this layout" or "I need to have lines without descenders that would bump into the other elements." Don't just choose all caps just because you don't know any better. The same thought applies to a centered arrangement; if you can put into words that you need a formal, sedate look for a project, then go ahead and use centered (and only centered!).

Letterhead&envelopes

Remember, your letterhead and envelopes should have the same basic layout as your business card. This provides your business with a cohesive look; when you give someone a business card today and next week send them a letter, you want to reinforce the image of your business. When you send a letter in an envelope with a business card enclosed, the three items should make a unified presentation of the professional level of your services.

To create such a unified presentation sometimes means changing your layout on one piece so it can accommodate the different shape of another piece of the package. That is, don't design your business card and get it printed until you have made sure that same basic arrangement will work on the collateral pieces.

These three pieces have no design relationship to each other: the letterhead is centered with pet on right; the envelope is flush left with pet on left; the business card is flush right.

Doggy's Best Friend
Boarding Kennels
Safe and Clean

123 South Frontage Road
Santa Fe, New Mexico 87505
v 505-555-5555 f 505-555-5550
ww.doggysbestfriend.com

Doggy's Best Friend
Boarding Kennels
Safe and Clean

123 South Frontage Road
Santa Fe, New Mexico 87505

Doggy's Best Friend
Boarding Kennels
Safe and Clean

123 South Frontage Road
Santa Fe, New Mexico 87505
v 505-555-5555 f 505-555-5550
ww.doggysbestfriend.com

Doggy's
Best Friend
Boarding Kennels
Safe and Clean

123 S. Frontage Road
Santa Fe
New Mexico
87505
505-555-5555 v
505-555-5550 f
www.doggysbestfriend.com

Doggy's
Best Friend
Boarding Kennels
Safe and Clean

123 S. Frontage Road
Santa Fe
New Mexico
87505

Doggy's
Best Friend
Boarding Kennels
Safe and Clean

123 S. Frontage Road
Santa Fe
New Mexico
87505
505-555-5555 v
505-555-5550 f
www.doggysbestfriend.com

These two sets of the same stationery each have a consistent look among the pieces; they have the same basic arrangement with adjustments in type size and spacing made for the different elements.

Type & body copy

There are lots of ways to indicate which numbers on the stationery or card are phone numbers, fax numbers, cell phone numbers, etc. On the opposite page we show you a variety of options.

And don't forget that the purpose of stationery is to write letters. Always keep in mind the body of the letter when you are designing the page; when you print a letter on that page, set it up to coordinate it with the layout. If you are creating this for a client, it's nice to show them a sample of how the body of a letter will appear—it can influence their decisions.

Numbers

Because there are typically quite a few numbers on a letterhead and business card, between the address, zip code, and all the phone numbers, it's nice to choose a typeface that has beautiful numbers built right into the face.

Most standard faces have regular, lining numbers, as shown below (lining numbers are all the same size, as opposed to oldstyle numbers as shown in the next column). If you use a face with lining numbers, make them at least a half-point or whole point smaller than the rest of the text; otherwise they overwhelm the line. Below, each example is 10-point type.

411 555 1234   Garamond

411 555 1234   Times

411 555 1234   Helvetica

If it works with your project, use a typeface with oldstyle numbers, as shown below. Oldstyle numbers are built like lowercase letters, with ascenders and descenders, so they fit right into a line of type. Below, the numbers are 10-point type. Compare them with the lining numbers in the previous column and notice how much more elegant and interesting these oldstyle numbers are.

411 505 1298   Golden Cockerel

411 505 1256   Dyadis OldStyle

411 505 5632   Highlander

411 505 5632   Bossa Nova

Descriptors

When you include telephone numbers, cell phone numbers, toll-free numbers, fax numbers, etc., on a letterhead or business card, it can be quite a challenge to label each of these numbers appropriately yet creatively.

Keep in mind that some items really don't need descriptive labels, such as a toll-free number—the 800 or 888 prefix tells us it's toll-free. However, if you are labeling every other number with its full descriptive name, be consistent and add the toll-free label.

Don't spell out the words telephone, facsimile, toll-free, etc., unless you have incorporated those words into your design. The initials shown below are easily understood. You might use V (voice), T (telephone) or P (phone), and C (cell). You really don't need to label obvious things like "email" or "web address" because their form makes it clear what they are; sometimes, however, the descriptive label can become part of the design.

p 411.505.1256		t e l e p h o n e
f 411.505.1257		411.505.1256
c 411.660.1258		c e l l p h o n e
		411.660.1257
V 411.505.1256		f a c s i m i l e
F 411.505.1257		411.505.1257
C 411.660.1258		t o l l f r e e
E jt@ratz.com		800.505.1212
		e m a i l
		jt@ratzcom
t: 411.505.1256		w e b a d d r e s s
f: 411.505.1257		www.ratz.com
e: jt@ratz.com		
w: www.ratz.com		*telephone*
		411 555 1234
		fax
		411 555 1234
ph 411.505.1256		*web*
fx 411.505.1257		www.ratz.com

Parentheses

There are a variety of alternatives to the parentheses that typically surround the area codes. On a clean page, parentheses tend to add clutter to the numbers unnecessarily. Below are alternatives to the parentheses around area codes.

411.505.1256	periods
411 505 5632	spaces
411-505-1256	hyphens

(you will probably have to use the baseline shift to move the hyphens up to where they belong)

[411] 505 5632	brackets
⁴¹¹ 505 5632	baseline shift
411 505 1256	italic area code
411/505.1256	slash
411 505.1256	**bold** vs. light
411 **505.1256**	light vs. **bold**

Letterhead body copy

Be conscious of where the body of a letter will appear on the stationery. Generally, using a little extra space between paragraphs (not a double return!) in the body creates a cleaner look instead of indenting each paragraph (and you know better than to use extra space *plus* an indent).

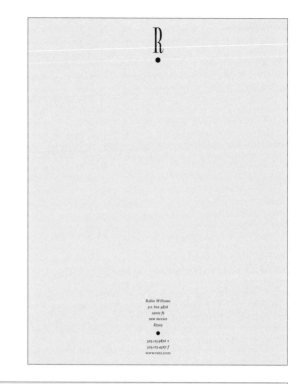

Don't be afraid to use small type or graphic elements. A business card or letterhead is not a book or even a brochure—it's a reference that is used for only seconds at a time so in this case, the initial visual impression is more important than sustained readability. (Although you will probably set the type a bit larger on the letterhead than you do on the business card.)

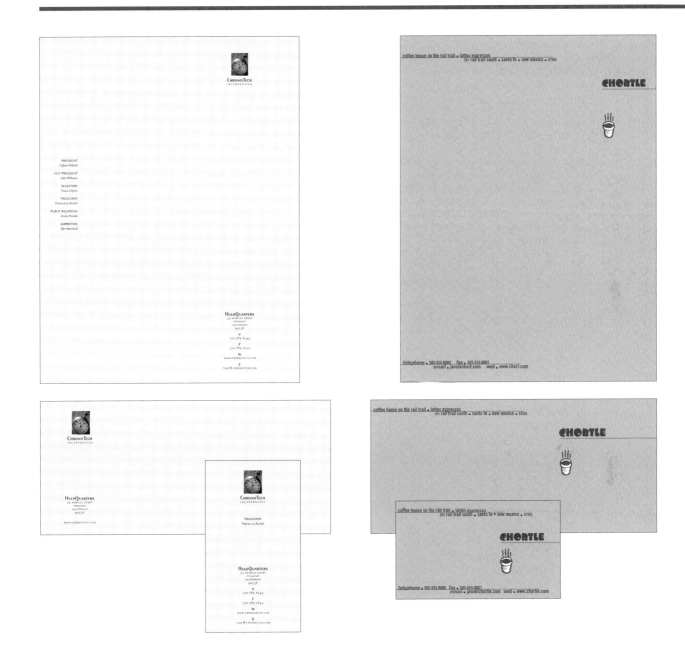

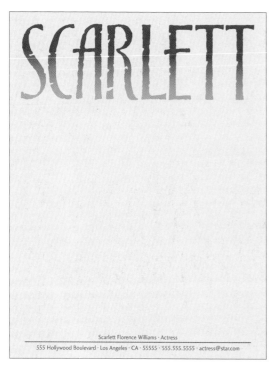

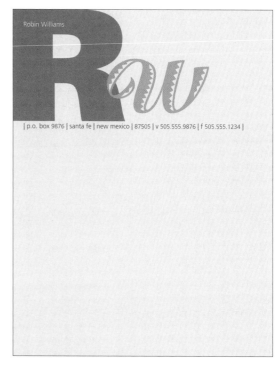

Don't be afraid to use large type or graphic elements. Most of us rarely write letters that fill all the available space on the page, so go ahead and be graphic. You can always use a second page for those occasions when you need more room to write.

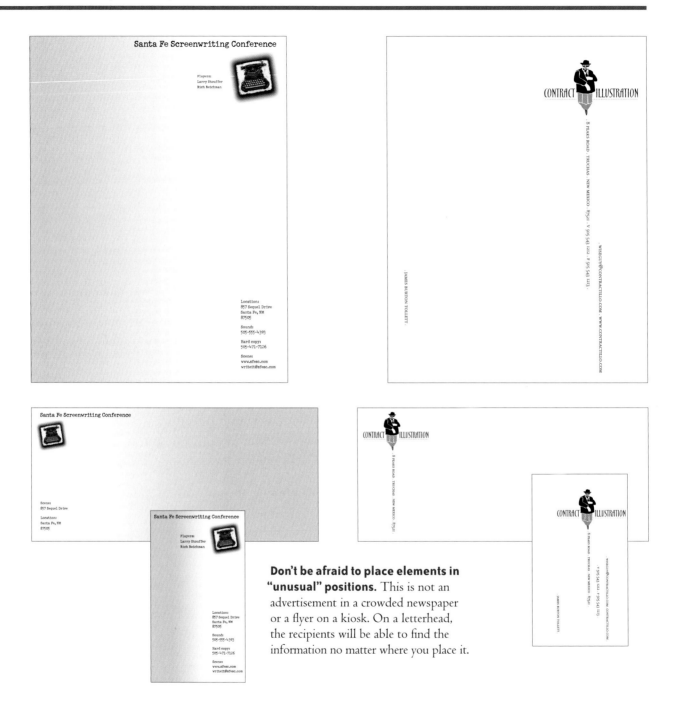

Don't be afraid to place elements in "unusual" positions. This is not an advertisement in a crowded newspaper or a flyer on a kiosk. On a letterhead, the recipients will be able to find the information no matter where you place it.

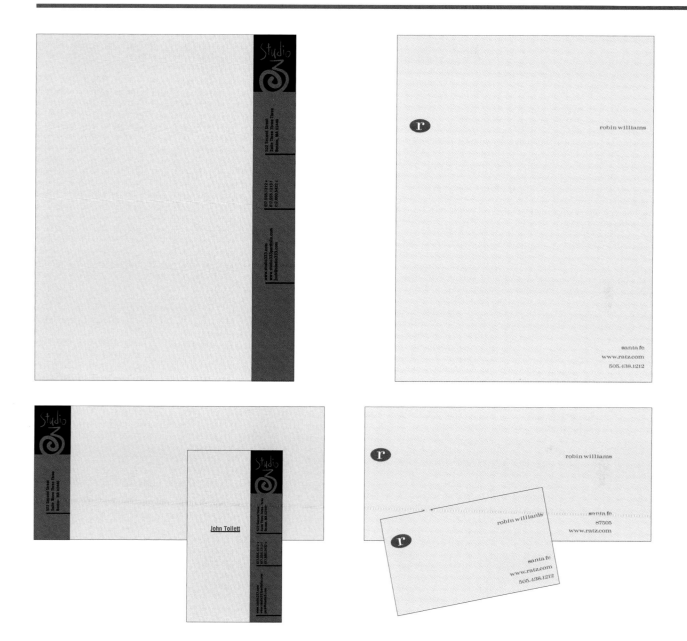

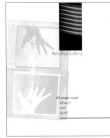

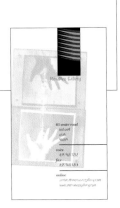

Don't be afraid to fill the writing space with an image—a light shade of an image, of course, so you can scrawl or print directly on top of it. Pull out and emphasize a piece of your logo, a different symbol of your business, or a photograph that is related to what you do. Let it bleed off the page (talk to the print shop first to see if that's an option on this job), let it fill the space, let it be dramatic! Remember, this is letterhead, not a billboard. The recipient will take the time to read what you write even if it is a wee bit less readable than type on a plain white background.

Letters&labels

Add a second page

When you print your letterhead package, you might consider printing fewer second pages at the same time. On the second page, you don't need all of the information that's on the cover page. A nice technique is to print just your logo, or even just a part of the logo. Or if you have a large image screened back on the first page, print that same image smaller on the second page, or maybe full strength but small. If your company uses a tag line, print just the tag line on the second page. Or pick up just one of the design elements from the cover page and print it on the second page.

Typically you will have five hundred or a thousand pieces printed of the first page of the letterhead, plus matching envelopes and business cards; print maybe one or two hundred of the second pages, depending on how often you think you'll use them.

Add a smaller letterhead

The standard stationery size that measures 8.5 x 11 is fine, but it's also nice to create a more personalized look on smaller paper. There are a number of standard but smaller sizes—check with your printer and ask what sizes they have and choose one that will fit neatly into a smaller envelope that the printer also has. Often a smaller letterhead, because it's more personal, doesn't carry all of the professional information that the regular business stationery does—your name and logo might be enough. Though it's a simpler layout, it should still tie in with your main pieces.

Print it yourself

Another simple and inexpensive solution is to design personal stationery on half of a regular sheet of paper. You can print two at a time on one sheet of paper, printed horizontal, then cut it. This size fits neatly into the size A4 envelope that you can buy at any office supply store.

Labels

If you plan to use labels, now is a good time to design and print them so a) they are consistent with your business package, and b) if you're using more than one color, you'll save money by printing everything at once.

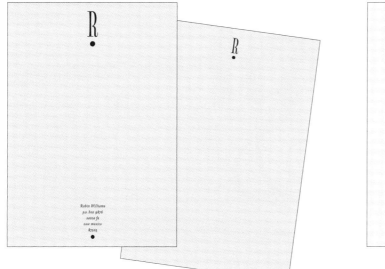

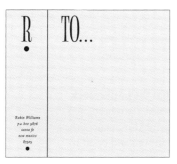

Above are smaller-sized, more personal letterhead examples that don't replace the formal letterheads, but complement them. They are shown here with examples of second pages. The designs for the second pages can also be used with the larger letterhead.

Left and right are examples of labels that coordinate with the business package. Labels can be just about any size and shape, but check with the printshop before you design them—they can help you determine the best size with the least amount of waste.

If you plan to print labels on your desktop printer, buy the labels first, then design to that size! Print a few samples onto plain paper to make sure they are positioned correctly on your page before running the labels through.

Examples

Below is a typical form. It's been used for years and so it's been refined to serve its purpose well—it just isn't very pretty. It doesn't take any longer to design a form that looks nice, so why not? This form doesn't use alignment to its advantage, nor contrast to call out important features, nor proximity to group similar elements together and separate others, nor repetition (consistency) to help create an organized, unified look. Also, it uses Courier in all caps. All caps can be nicely done, as we discussed in Chapter 7, but they should never be used just because you don't know any better.

All we did in this version shown below is change everything from all caps to regular lowercase letters with beginning caps (called "sentence caps"). It's already easier to read. But is there any reason to use Courier in a form like this? Not really. Courier is not only a little more difficult to read than most faces because it is monospaced, but it instantly projects an unsophisticated form (there are ways to use Courier and have the page look trendy, but that can only happen if the rest of the page is well designed).

Form 1 (left):

ASTA MAÑANA HIGH SCHOOL
MEDICAL INFORMATION
MEDICAL RELEASE

STUDENT_____
ID _____ DATE OF BIRTH _____
☐ SR ☐ JR ☐ SPH ☐ FSH

☐ FIELD TRIP   ☐ ONE DAY
☐ ACTIVITY TRIP   ☐ EXTENDED

ORGANIZATION/ACADEMIC CLASS _____

EMERGENCY		FATHER/GUARDIAN	MOTHER/GUARDIAN	EMERGENCY CONTACT PERSON
	NAME			
	ADDRESS			
	H PHONE			
	W PHONE			

PERSON RESPONSIBLE FOR MEDICAL EXPENSES:

INSURANCE	COMPANY	PLAN NUMBER
	ADDRESS	GROUP NAME/NUMBER
		INSURED ID NUMBER

MEDICAL

ALLERGIES _____
DATE LAST TETANUS SHOT _____
STATE PHYSICAL RESTRICTIONS, HEART CONDITION, DIABETES, ASTHMA, EPILEPSY, RHEUMATIC FEVER, OR OTHER EXISTING MEDICAL CONDITIONS _____

MEDICATIONS CURRENTLY TAKING _____

LIABILITY RELEASE   THE ASTA MAÑANA PUBLIC SCHOOLS, THEIR REPRESENTATIVES, AGENTS, AND EMPLOYEES ARE RELEASED FROM LIABILITIES OF INJURY TO THE STUDENT EXCEPT FOR INJURY OR DAMAGE RESULTING FROM WILLFUL NEGLIGENT ACTION OF THE ASTA MAÑANA PUBLIC SCHOOLS, THEIR REPRESENTATIVES, AGENTS, AND EMPLOYEES.

PARENTAL PERMISSION TO OBTAIN MEDICAL SERVICES   IN CASE OF ACCIDENT OR MEDICAL EMERGENCY, THE ABOVE MENTIONED SPONSOR IS GIVEN PERMISSION TO OBTAIN MEDICAL CARE FOR STUDENT.

SIGNATURES   WE HAVE READ, AGREE WITH, AND WILL FOLLOW ALL OF THE ABOVE.

_____   _____
STUDENT   DATE   PARENT/GUARDIAN   DATE

Form 2 (right):

Asta Mañana High School
Medical Information
Medical Release

Student_____
ID _____ Date of Birth _____
☐ Sr ☐ Jr ☐ Sph ☐ Fsh

☐ Field Trip   ☐ One Day
☐ Activity Trip   ☐ Extended

Organization/Academic Class _____

EMERGENCY		Father/Guardian	Mother/Guardian	Emergency Contact Person
	Name			
	Address			
	H Phone			
	W Phone			

Person responsible for medical expenses:

INSURANCE	Company	Plan Number
	Address	Group Name/Number
		Insured ID Number

MEDICAL

Allergies _____
Date Last Tetanus Shot _____
State physical restrictions, heart condition, diabetes, asthma, epilepsy, rheumatic fever, or other existing medical conditions _____

Medications currently taking _____

Liability release   The Asta Mañana Public Schools, their representatives, agents, and employees are released from liabilities of injury to the student except for injury or damage resulting from willful negligent action of the Asta Mañana Public Schools, their representatives, agents, and employees.

Parental Permission to obtain medical services   In case of accident or medical emergency, the above mentioned sponsor is given permission to obtain medical care for student.

Signatures   We have read, agree with, and will follow all of the above.

_____   _____
Student   Date   Parent/Guardian   Date

Form 1 (left):

Asta Mañana High School
Medical Information
Medical Release

Student_____
ID_____ Date of Birth_____
☐ Sr ☐ Jr ☐ Sph ☐ Fsh

☐ Field Trip   ☐ One Day
☐ Activity Trip   ☐ Extended

Organization/Academic Class _____

EMERGENCY		Father/Guardian	Mother/Guardian	Emergency Contact Person
	Name			
	Address			
	H Phone			
	W Phone			
	Person responsible for medical expenses:			

INSURANCE			
	Company	Plan Number	
	Address	Group Name/Number	
		Insured ID Number	

MEDICAL

Allergies _____
Date Last Tetanus Shot _____
State physical restrictions, heart condition, diabetes, asthma, epilepsy, rheumatic fever, or other existing medical conditions _____

Medications currently taking _____

Liability release The Asta Mañana Public Schools, their representatives, agents, and employees are released from liabilities of injury to the student except for injury or damage resulting from willful negligent action of the Asta Mañana Public Schools, their representatives, agents, and employees.

Parental Permission to obtain medical services In case of accident or medical emergency, the above mentioned sponsor is given permission to obtain medical care for student.

Signatures We have read, agree with, and will follow all of the above.

_____   _____
Student   Date   Parent/Guardian   Date

Form 2 (right):

Asta Mañana High School
Medical Information
Medical Release

Student _____
ID _____ Date of Birth _____
☐ Senior ☐ Junior ☐ Sophomore ☐ Freshman

☐ Field Trip   ☐ One Day
☐ Activity Trip ☐ Extended

Organization/Academic Class_____

EMERGENCY		Father/Guardian	Mother/Guardian	Emergency Contact
	Name			
	Address			
	Home Phone			
	Work Phone			
	Person responsible for medical expenses:			

INSURANCE			
	Company	Plan Number	
	Address	Group Name/Number	
		Insured ID Number	

MEDICAL

Allergies _____

Date of last Tetanus shot _____

State physical restrictions, heart condition, diabetes, asthma, epilepsy, rheumatic fever, or other existing medical conditions _____

Medications currently taking _____

Liability release: The Asta Mañana Public Schools, their representatives, agents, and employees are released from liabilities of injury to the student except for injury or damage resulting from willful negligent action of the Asta Mañana Public Schools, their representatives, agents, and employees.

Parental Permission to obtain medical services: In case of accident or medical emergency, the above-mentioned sponsor is given permission to obtain medical care for the student.
Signatures: We have read, agree with, and will follow all of the above.

_____   _____
Student   Date   Parent/Guardian   Date

Above, we changed the typeface to a sans serif for the titles in the boxes, and a serif face for the paragraphs of text at the bottom of the form. Now we can look at the alignments. Can you see places where items could be aligned? Do you see inconsistencies, like the spaces between the lines and the text? Do you see places where we could add contrast to help guide the user through the form, point out important areas, and make the page more visually interesting along the way?

If you think the form is eventually going to get reproduced from a copy of a copy of a copy, as often happens, avoid using any screens behind words (the pale tints of color, as above) because they get clogged up and messy if reproduced on copy machines or fax machines. If you do need to put a screen behind text, make sure the text is a little bolder than normal.

Now that we've got good typefaces in sentence case, we can clean up the rest of the form:

> **Contrast:** We set important words in the heavy version of the sans serif to help guide the user through the form, as well as make it more visually attractive. We turned the three headings along the left on their sides to make them easier to read and gave them more contrast as well. **Do not** use an underline to emphasize words!

> **Repetition:** We made the spacing consistent. The contrast also creates a repetitive effect, as does the alignment.

> **Alignment:** This simple technique instantly makes the form neater. You can see that every element now has some visual connection with something else on the page—nothing is placed arbitrarily.

> **Proximity:** The elements that belong together are connected in neat units.

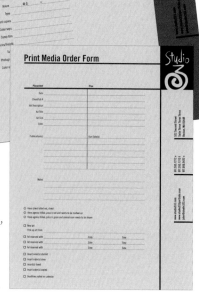

All you need are the basic principles

The basic principles outlined on the previous page apply to every form. Forms typically don't need clever copy (although some would benefit from it!), illustrations, or photographs, so you are down to the simple task of making it attractive (so the user will feel comfortable) and practical (so the user can fill it out without difficulty).

If you are printing in-house forms or a collection of forms for a client at the same time that you print their other material, such as business cards and letterhead, then it won't cost much extra to print the forms in color. But most forms don't need any color at all, or you will perhaps print them directly from your computer as you need them—as shown to the right, a form can be just as attractive without your company colors.

This form is "black-and-white," meant to be printed as needed directly from the computer. It is printed onto paper stock that matches the company letterhead.

Clarity

If you have many lines of data, as on an order form or financial chart, using a color tint on alternating lines helps clarify the information. You can create these colored bars easily using the "paragraph rules" feature in your page-layout program: as you type, the bars appear automatically (above, below, or behind the line of type), you can control the spacing between them and their length with single clicks. If your application has a table feature, that makes it even easier!

Book	Editions
Sweet Swan of Avon: Did a Woman Write Shakespeare?	
Macs on the Go: Mobile Computing Guide*	
Mac OS X 10.4 Tiger: Peachpit Learning Series	
Robin Williams Cool Mac Apps Book*	2 editions
The Little Mac Book	8 editions
The Little Mac OS X Book	
The Little Mac Book	Tiger edition
The Little Mac Book	Panther Edition
Robin Williams Mac OS X Book*	Panther edition
Robin Williams Mac OS X Book	Jaguar edition
The Little Mac iApps Book*	
Top Ten Reasons Robin Loves OS X	
The Little iMac Book	3 editions
The Little iBook Book*	
Windows for Mac Users	
The Non-Designer's Design Book	2 editions
The Non-Designer's Web Book*	3 editions
The Non-Designer's Type Book	3 editions
The Non-Designer's Scan and Print Book*	
The Non-Designer's Guerrilla Marketing Guide*	
Robin Williams Design Workshop*	2 editions
Robin Williams Web Design Workshop*	2 editions
Robin Williams DVD Design Workshop*	
The Mac is Not a Typewriter	2 editions
The PC is not a typewriter	
PageMaker 4/5: An Easy Desk Reference	3 editions
Tabs and Indents on the Macintosh	
Jargon: an informal dictionary of computer terms	
How to Boss Your Fonts Around	2 editions
A Blip in the Continuum	Mac and Windows editions
Home Sweet Home Page	2 editions
Beyond The Little Mac Book	
Beyond The Mac is not a typewriter	

Carnation
Used for wreaths and garlands; often a reference to middle age because they bloom in midsummer.

Crab (crab apple)
A small apple with a delicate flavor and pink-and-white blossoms, often roasted and set afloat in a bowl of ale or wassail.

Cowslip
A favorite flower of fairies, used as their drinking cups. Used for making wine, the leaves for salad, the juice for coughs.

Daisy
The flower of the month of April; in England the daisy is small, white, and covers grassy slopes and fields.

Fennel
Fennel smells like licorice; it is the emblem of flattery. An English country proverb states, "Sow fennel, sow sorrow."

Gillyvor
Flowers of mixed colors in the carnation family; often a reference to middle age because they bloom in midsummer.

Lady-smock
Also known as cuckoo flower; blooms in meadows, covering grass like smocks laid out to dry, in early spring when the first notes of the cuckoo are heard.

Marigold
Also known as Mary-buds; used in salads, as ointment for skin, in lotions for sprains; petals in broth "comfort the heart."

Pansy
The names comes from the French pensée, which means "thought." Ophelia says, "... and there is pansies, that's for thoughts."

Pink
The smallest member of the carnation family; often used to describe perfect manners, as in "the very pink of courtesy."

Primrose and violets
Both flowers bloom so early in the spring that they don't live to see the summer sun; often associated with death.

Rosemary
An herb known for faithfulness and remembrance, as well as memory (tuck a sprig behind your ear while studying). Thick stems were used to make lutes.

Rue
An herb with a strong smell and bitter, sour flavor; associated with repentance, pity, grace, and forgiveness (often placed beside judges in court)

Thyme
Symbol of sweetness; often planted in garden paths so walking upon it will release the scent.

Woodbine (honeysuckle)
Symbol of affection and faithfulness; a creeping, climbing plant that twines its vines around trees and posts.

Spreadsheet or database forms

Many in-house forms are more useful as computer spreadsheets or databases where the data can be entered directly on the computer and output as hard copy, rather than handwriting on the printed form. You don't have to be an expert with a program like Excel or FileMaker Pro to create a simple form—try an application like AppleWorks, Pages, Mariner Write, Microsoft Word, or even Mariner Calc. They allow you to set up the labels as well as the empty spaces you'll fill in. You can use any typeface you want, align elements, add graphics, and more, almost as you would in a page-layout application. The same basic design rules apply!

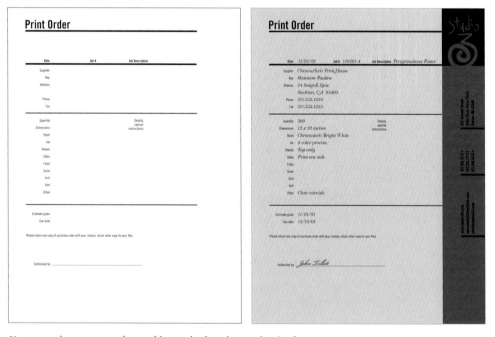

You can easily set up a simple spreadsheet or database that matches (fairly well) your other business pieces. Save the form as a template so every time you open it, it will be empty of data. Enter your new data into the empty cells or fields. You can either print it onto blank stationery (as shown above-right) or add your logo and other pertinent information directly on the computer form and print onto plain paper.

Web site forms

As much as possible, web site forms should follow the same basic principles as print forms: **contrast** so the visitor can figure out what's going on; **repetition** (consistency) so they don't get confused; **alignment** to keep things organized and clear; and **proximity** to make sure related elements are near each other and disparate elements are separated by a little extra space—those spatial relationships communicate huge amounts to the reader.

If you have nice, clean alignments in your web form, you won't need to turn on those awful borders, as shown above, left. Instead of the borders, let your column alignments create the edges, and use color to separate items, as shown above, right.

These labels are aligned left, and the fields have a strong left edge. But between the labels and the fields is all that wobbly space. When you have two strong edges, put them together, as in the arrangement above: strong right against the strong left. And align the heading!

*Any form will look clean and professional if you just line things up. Notice the labels above (Name, Address, etc.) are aligned on their **right** edges so they provide a strong, solid line against the **left** edges of the empty fields. This strengthens the entire piece, as opposed to the arrangement shown below.*

Ideas

So there is no excuse for bad-looking or difficult-to-use forms! Here are some ideas that will not only make a form look nicer, but will make it easier to use.

Lines

The lines on a form do not have to be heavy, black lines! The purpose of the line is merely to give the user a guideline for where to write. Heavy lines often obscure the handwritten information. Here are some options (be sure to leave enough room in which to write!):

Thin lines

Name

Company

Address

City   State   Zip

Thicker, gray lines

Name

Company

Address

City   State   Zip

Dotted lines

Name

Company

Address

City   State   Zip

Dashed lines

Name

Company

Address

City   State   Zip

Thicker, lightly colored lines

Name

Company

Address

City   State   Zip

Boxes

If you set a box around a field, please leave enough room in which to write! Here are several options for boxes:

| Name |
| Company |
| Address |
| City | State | Zip |

| Name |
| Company |
| Address |
| City | State | Zip |

| Name |
| Company |
| Address |
| City | State | Zip |

| Name |
| Company |
| Address |
| City | State | Zip |

Checkboxes

You have more options than just the standard empty checkbox. Even if you need a fairly traditional look to your form, you can still get away with using circles or triangles instead of squares. If you can use a more playful look, try some of the characters in the fonts Zapf Dingbats, Wingdings, or Webdings, which are probably already on your computer; outline them with a thin line so a user can fill in the empty space.

If your logo or symbol associated with your business is appropriate, perhaps use that (or a piece of it) outlined as a checkbox. Or use a playful image that has something to do with your company or the purpose of the form, like a dog bone or beachball.

Please send me:	**Bill me:**
☐ Carnations	○ Visa
☐ Crab apples	○ MasterCard
☐ Cowslips	○ American Express
☐ Daisies	○ Discover

Please send me:	**Please send me:**
▽ Carnations	◇ Carnations
▽ Crab apples	◇ Crab apples
▽ Cowslips	◇ Cowslips
▽ Daisies	◇ Daisies

Please send me:	**Please send me:**
‹ › Carnations	✷ Carnations
‹ › Crab apples	✷ Crab apples
‹ › Cowslips	✷ Cowslips
‹ › Daisies	✷ Daisies

Please send me:	**Please send me:**
[ ] Carnations	Carnations
[ ] Crab apples	Crab apples
[ ] Cowslips	Cowslips
[ ] Daisies	Daisies

Sometimes you might have items on your form where the user can check more than one box, and other items where the user must choose only one of the options. Use the standard boxes we are accustomed to seeing on our computers: checkboxes for multiple choices; radio buttons for one choice. Of course, you might need an explanation on your form for those users who would be unfamiliar with this convention, something simple like "Choose one of the following" or "Choose as many as you like of the following."

131

Look around

Deductions

Please enter your deductions for this filing period in the fields below. The total amount of your deductions will appear on Line 3 in the next step.

« Previous | Step 2 of 8 | Next »

DEDUCTIONS	SALES AMOUNT	USE AMOUNT
Line B - Food Stamp and W.I.C Sales		
Line C - Sales for Resale		500
Line D - Prescription Drugs		100
Line E - Returned Goods		200
Line F - Feed, Seed and Fertilizer		300
Line G - Bad Debts		400
Line H - Sales to U.S. Government		500
Line I - Farm Machinery		600
Line J - Sales to Hospitals and Organizations Exempt by Statute (See GR31)		700
Line K - Sales to Direct Pay Permit Holders		800
Line L - 38% of Gross Selling Price on New Manufactured/Mobile Homes		90
Line M - Used Manufactured/Mobile Homes		100
Line N - Other Legal Deductions		100
		100
TOTALS		100
		$4,590.00

Unless you are on a mission to research forms, you probably don't even notice them. If you never plan to create one, skip this exercise (although we suspect if you are even reading this chapter, a form-to-be has come into your life, like it or not).

Designer Exercise: Keep your eyes open for forms and invoices—at the dentist's office, backs of magazines, in the mail, or stop by the local IRS office. If in your first glance you are impressed with the look and design of the form, put into words exactly what gives you that feeling. If you are not impressed, put into words why not—we guarantee one or more of the very basic principles of design are missing (and the form probably uses a 12-point font that comes with the computer). Remember, you are looking not only for good design, but how well the designer was able to integrate good looks with functionality.

9. Advertising

Advertising is a big subject. There are many books, courses, and seminars about advertising and its related areas—copywriting, marketing, sales, etc. In this chapter, we're going to focus simply on what it looks like. If a reader's attention is not drawn to the ad in the first place, it doesn't matter what the copy says or how well it's marketed.

A clever headline that's short enough to be read at a glance may be able to captivate a reader, but it's usually the power of design, or the visual, that stops someone long enough to read a headline.

Black-and-white ads

Where do you start when a client or your business needs an ad? First of all, read some books on advertising and marketing. Then make it visually attractive, keeping in mind the marketing precepts.

Often you'll be given specifications for an ad, such as the size that the budget will allow, whether it's color or black and white, whether you can afford original or stock photography or illustration, and all those other things we talked about in Chapter 4. So the conditions of all these specs end up making half of your design decisions for you.

If you've been handed body copy and head-lines and told to design around them, that's another limitation that automatically cuts out some options, both conceptual and creative. If it's your responsibility to come up with the idea, then your creative job is easier but your creative freedom is larger (and thus more overwhelming), also.

It's sometimes easier to create your own concept and copy built around a visual that you find or an idea that you have than it is to effectively design around a copywriter's drydullboring copy. For instance, the ad on the right has nothing going for it in the way of concept. But you can still make it look good and capture attention.

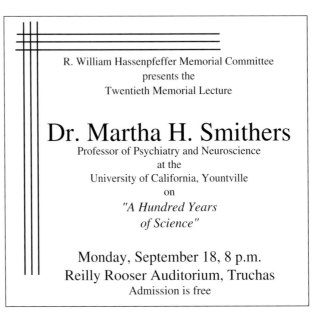

R. William Hassenpfeffer Memorial Committee
presents the
Twentieth Memorial Lecture

Dr. Martha H. Smithers
Professor of Psychiatry and Neuroscience
at the
University of California, Yountville
on
*"A Hundred Years
of Science"*

Monday, September 18, 8 p.m.
Reilly Rooser Auditorium, Truchas
Admission is free

It's not bad

At least the designer of this ad was conscious about the line breaks (where the sentences end so you don't have an odd word hanging at the end of the line). We know they were trying to add a graphic sort of element when they stuck those arbitary lines in the corner, but really, *it's okay for the corners to be empty.* They don't mind at all. And we know the designer must have *some* other font besides Times Roman.

This ad gets the point across, and the fact that it's rather dull is not going to stop anyone from going to this partic-ular lecture. But there are many ads just this boring that will definitely affect business—you might have the juiciest goodies in your shop downtown, but if your ad is dull, people automatically assume your shop goodies are dull.

R. William Hassenpfeffer Memorial Committee
presents the Twentieth Memorial Lecture

Dr. Martha H. Smithers

Professor of Psychiatry and Neuroscience
at the University of California, Yountville
will be speaking on the topic of

A Hundred Years of Science

Monday, September 18, 8 p.m.
Reilly Rooser Auditorium, Truchas
Admission is free

A Hundred Years of Science

Dr. Martha H. Smithers
Professor of Psychiatry and Neuroscience
at the University of California, Yountville

Monday, September 18, 8 P.M.
Reilly Rooser Auditorium, Truchas
Admission is free

This Twentieth Memorial Lecture is presented
by the R. William Hassenpfeffer Memorial Committee

Prioritize the information. What is the most important item; what is it that will make a reader's eyes stop on the ad? That item should be your focal point, either by size, placement, or its intriguing image. The original ad did a pretty good job of prioritizing; they just need to push it a little more, make the focal point stronger.

Choose a nice typeface. Basically, choose anything that is not built into your computer. Particularly avoid Helvetica/Arial, Times/Times New Roman, and Palatino/Book Antiqua. Buy some new fonts! They're not that expensive and they make a world of difference in anything you do.

If you want to use more than one typeface, in a piece make sure to choose fonts that do not look similar to each other! If they are not the same family, make sure they contrast with strength. Contrast their size, weight, structure, form, direction, and color.

Prioritize the information. This is just an example of emphasizing a different priority. What becomes the focal point depends entirely on what you think will draw a reader's eye to the ad. If you can get a reader's eyes to the ad, they will read the smaller copy if they're interested. If you can't get them to the ad at all, it doesn't matter how large you make the supplementary information like the date and time.

Let the white space be there.

Focal point

What is the focal point? In this ad, will most people recognize the speaker's name? The photograph? Will "revival services" be what stops readers so they read the ad? Is the word "featuring" really as important as everything else in the headline? Figure out what the focus is and focus on it. Let everything else be subordinate.

Get rid of superfluous stuff

Go through every word in your advertisement and remove anything superfluous. This includes items like "NM," as in the ad to the right. Since this piece appears in the local newspaper and the town is listed (and the town is in the middle of the state), there is no danger anyone might end up in the wrong state to attend the meetings. How about the endings of the numbers (like 8th)—are they really necessary? Do you have to abbreviate the street name? It creates a messy little spot with the period and the comma; although it takes more space to spell out the name, it looks neater.

Does this piece really need a double rule around it? Use the layout and headline to call attention to the ad; don't clutter it up with extraneous, useless lines.

Revival Services Featuring Internet Evangelist Url Ratz

Friday, August 8th
10:30 am to 7:30 pm
Saturday, August 9th
through Wednesday, August 13th
6:00 Nightly

Url's Internet Cafe
123 Montezuma Ave., Santa Fe, NM
Where the Internet is Changing People's Lives

Childcare will be Provided   Interpretacion en Español

Crop the photo

In a small ad like this one, if there is superfluous space around a photo, get rid of it. Sometimes extra space in a photo is an artistic technique, but in this case, it's not.

Start with the basic principles

You may decide you want to break the rules—that's great, but you have to know the rules before you can break them. Use **contrast** to create a focal point and visual interest. Use **repetition** to tie the elements together. Use **alignment** to organize both the information and the white space. Use **proximity** to group elements together and separate elements that are not part of the unit.

Alignment

Draw a line through the centers of each of these units. Is there any connection between them? Now, if you aligned each of these elements on a strong flush left, you would have a cleaner piece, even though each element would still have a different left alignment. You can get away with a variety of flush edges but not with centered elements: we *see* the line down the strong flush left edge, but we *don't* see the line down the center—we see the soft edges. The strength of a left or right alignment lends strength to the page, while the weakness of the soft edge of a centered alignment is made even weaker when there are multiples of them.

Proximity

In this group, the line "10:30 am to 7:30 pm" is just as close to the next line, "Saturday, August 9th" as it is to the line above it. This can create confusion as to the exact time and date of the meeting. The principle of proximity clears this up—the elements that belong together should be tucked closely together, and the spacing between elements indicates their relationships. That is, there should be a wee bit of space between the two different time frames, and even more space between the time frames and the place.

Do not use the same amount of space between every item! The spatial relationships communicate to us instantly; they tell us what is important, what is functional, etc.

White space

Look at the white space in this ad. It's all broken up, chunks of it are scattered everywhere. When you follow the basic design principles, the white space will automatically end up, neatly organized, where it should be. It is your job to *let it be there*.

Revival Services
featuring Internet Evangelist

Url Ratz

Url's Internet Cafe
Where the Internet is Changing People's Lives

123 Montezuma Avenue, Santa Fe

All day: Friday, August 8
10:30 A.M. to 7:30 P.M.

Every night: Saturday, August 9 thru
Wednesday, August 13
6 P.M.

Childcare will be provided
Interpretacion en Español

Contrast

To create the focal point, we used **contrast.** In this particular case, the photograph of the famous evangelist is so well known that we made it the most prominent, as well as his name. Everything else is subordinate. If a reader's eyes are pulled into the ad through the photograph and headline name, they will read the rest of the body copy, even if we made it 5-point type. But if we set everything large and in similar sizes, a reader's eyes will just glaze over the ad. Suck the reader in with the main point.

Notice the **white space!** In a busy newspaper, your eyes are pulled toward the peaceful white space. Let it be there. White space is on sale today.

Check the **alignments.** Every element is aligned in some way with something else on the page.

Check the **proximity** of elements to each other, and the spatial relationships between everything.

Check the **repetition** of fonts, weights, lines, and alignments.

Type choice tip

You'll notice that for black-and-white ads throughout this chapter we usually use fairly strong typefaces instead of delicate faces with thin strokes. This is because black-and-white ads are often destined for newspapers, newsletters, or inexpensive souvenir programs where quality control can sometimes be unpredicatable, or at the least, it's printed onto absorbent paper. If a black-and-white ad is placed in a glossy, high-quality magazine, fine lettering isn't a problem.

But most clients want the ad to work in all environments, so avoiding some fonts that may fall apart at small sizes can save you headaches and grief. We also try not to get extreme with small type, especially small type on a black background, unless we are very confident in the printing quality and paper stock that will be used.

Some design firms win awards with teeny-type layouts, but remember, these awards are given by other designers, not people who are reading the ads. Several years back, a dog food packaging project won lots of fancy design awards, but it didn't sell the dog food—the huge bags of designer-label dog food just didn't go over well in the feed stores.

This headline for a crane service adds an element of fun and is meant to catch the reader's attention with humor. We started by placing the elements in the space, like spreading out the pieces of a jigsaw puzzle onto the kitchen table. At least one of the photos needs to be large to convey the feeling of massive boulders. The head-line is long so we limited our headline type choices to those that were bold and condensed.

Reversing the headline out of a black box makes it appear even bolder and creates a nice, strong contrast with the bottom half of the ad, as well as with the space around it on the magazine page. We added the smaller inset photo so we could actually show the crane and for the dramatic effect of showing a huge bolder in mid-air.

Next we started refining the headline to give it more impact and size contrast. This enabled us to make the catch-line ("Payback Time")

twice as large. The rest of the headline, even though it's smaller than before, stands out more because it's more isolated, more in contrast. This contrast of sizes also presented some design opportunities for stacking and tucking type in a visually interesting way.

We reworded the headline slightly so we could break it into two separate sentences. In the second version, we tried pulling the bottom of the black background up to the top of the photo,

but eventually moved it back down and put a white border around the photo to separate it from the background. In the final version we added a black bar across the bottom of the ad (repetition) to balance the heavy black weight at the top of the ad, and to tie the whole piece together.

The body copy is set in a casual font to reflect the tone of the copy. As a final touch we used a version of the logo that becomes a typographic visual pun.

A jumble of words contrasting with so much white space makes this ad impossible to ignore. Deviating from convention and placing the logo at the top of the ad (instead of the standard position at the bottom) leaves a stark, empty space in which the brief message and contact information can stand out.

Sometimes it's difficult to get a client to accept white space—they often feel that if they're paying for the space, they want to fill it up. Tell the client that white space was on sale this week and you got a good price on it.

The provocative image and the extreme left-dominant composition of the photograph made this flush-left layout a natural solution—if there is already a strength in one element of the layout, follow that strength, play it up! If the main element is a tall, vertical image, strengthen that tall, vertical by making the entire ad or poster tall.

We didn't want to diminish the extreme contrast of the stark white and the blacks and grays in the image, so we set the text and border in a medium gray. The client name in black creates a nice contrast with the rest of the type so it stands out, and also acts as a repetition of the black in the photo to tie the two elements together.

The headline ("scandalous") presents a conceptual contrast between the formality and sedate feeling created by the typeface, size, and color, contrasted with the mayhem and distaste associated with the word itself.

Don't you just hate traveling with large groups?

Same here.

Peregrinations
GLOBAL TRAVEL
www.peregrinationsgt.com

Don't you just hate traveling with large groups?

Same here.

Peregrinations
GLOBAL TRAVEL
www.peregrinationsgt.com

Never underestimate the power of a typeface to communicate something more than the words.

The visual you choose to use can influence your approach to a design. The vertical shape of the photograph led us to design this poster using an extreme vertical layout, shown to the left (when you have a strength in an element, play up that strength; in this case, the strong, tall, vertical). The condensed headline face, stacked in five lines, emphasizes the vertical visual impact. The unusual shape captures attention, either as an ad or as an unusual poster shape.

For a more conventional poster, or to fit into a more conventional ad space, we created the variation you see above. We made the photo as large as possible, and repeated the basic shape of the image in the headline.

Clients are often squeamish about using such abbreviated body copy, but most clients that have a web site can appreciate the value of using the print ad space to create a memorable impression, while letting the web site give the potential customers access to complete details and rich content.

This is the original stock photo.

This is a case of letting a stock photo do all the work for you. Originally the photograph had a couple of barn silhouettes in it. We realized that it would be very easy to delete those barns and add whatever silhouette we wanted. We didn't want to cover up the sun glare so the only place we could put Url Ratz was on the right. That dictated that the headline should go directly above and lead down to the silhouette. After that is was irresistible to add the callout in the middle of the glare.

Don't worry if you don't approach a design challenge with a fully realized solution before you get to the computer. As you may have already discovered, playing with the elements directly on the screen makes solutions appear that you didn't have in your head before you started.

This is also an example of creating a single solution (although separate computer files) of the same ad to work in both black and white as well as color. Because this particular photo so clearly evokes a sunset, our minds actually sort of "see" the color in the gray values.

Color ads

The visual impact of color is powerful and seductive. You can use it in large or small doses with equal effectiveness. Color ad space is available in a variety of sizes and shapes, creating a visual playground for designers.

The psychology of color is important and it varies from culture to culture, but most of us rely on instinct and our own personal reactions when choosing particular colors for projects. It's probably safe to assume that *your* reaction to color will be an average reaction in this country, but if you are doing international work, read some color studies.

Keep in mind the principles of contrast, alignment, and visual impact and you can create a visually compelling color ad.

This is the original stock image.

Here's another example of building an ad idea around a stock image that is guaranteed to catch attention and then finding a way to relate it to the client's message.

This conservative, centered layout uses a unique headline placement for visual interest and to create a visual tie-in with the highly decorative illustration. We selected colors from the illustration to create the color blends in the background rectangles, leaving a light-colored area for the body copy. The beautiful stock illustration and the unusual, curved headline make for an ad with high visibility.

Design variations that you experiment with *after* you've developed a usable layout usually lead to the final version that works best. Digital tools and techniques make design experimentation feasible, even with very tight deadline constraints. Small revisions and fine tuning can make a big visual difference.

The example directly above contains some nice elements, but it appears to be a hodge-podge of text and logos.

This version organizes the disparate elements better by containing all of the body copy in a background shape, reducing the size of the headline, rearranging it slightly, and repeating the rough-edged shape behind the subhead at the top of the ad.

The final version adds subtle visual interest by decreasing the width of the copy's background shape so that the petroglyph logo can break out of the box and into the white space. Having the text break away from the background color helps to give a spontaneous, casual, and fun feeling to the ad.

We placed the date into an organic shape to give it more prominence and to repeat the organic shape theme.

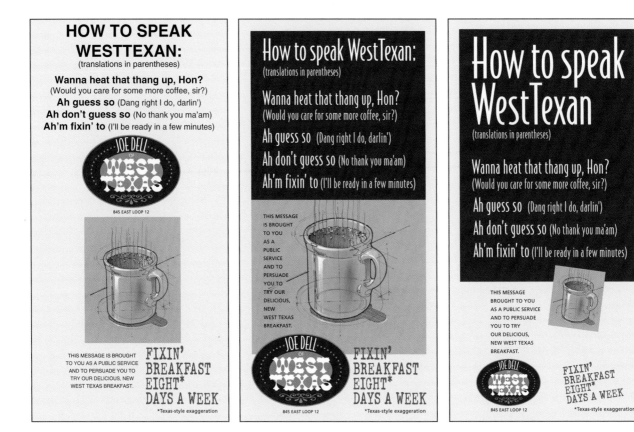

The regional personality of this cafe is reflected in an ad for a local visitors guide. The first version is little more than copy and graphic elements spread around in the ad space. The humorous copy is fun, but the layout does not attract a reader's eyes.

Above, we've added a lot of contrast by reversing the lengthy headline copy out of a dark box. We made the ad more attractive by using an earthy color for the background, which makes the logo's key words pop out in better contrast.

We'd be happy with this version except we know from experience that it's always worth trying one more variation. Also, we begin to notice that all separate elements of the ad are rather large and so they compete for visual focus—something needs to be the boss. We need to decide what is most important and let that element become a focal point.

The coffee cup illustration is interesting, but we'd rather make sure you see the headline. In the version above, the first part of the headline is visually dominant. The smaller size of the other elements not only allows the headline to become a focal point, it also creates better contrast and allows for a less crowded and more casual look to the entire piece.

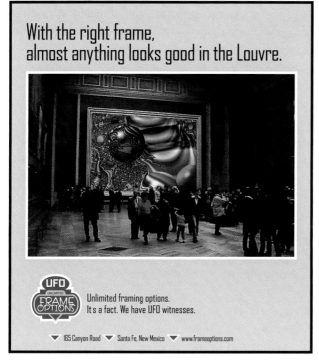

When creating a concept, consider combining two unrelated images or concepts into one for an attention-getting visual. The layout of the ad is quite simple (flush left), but the image is compelling and its relative size to the rest of the ad creates a great visual impact.

Incongruity can grab attention. The conceptual contrast between the computer-generated image and the uninformed quote in the headline delivers a message that computer art has come of age. The out-of-alignment typography continues the contradictory theme. The overlapping of the oversized quote marks and image creates a single visual impression that's separated by a generous amount of white space from the client information at the bottom.

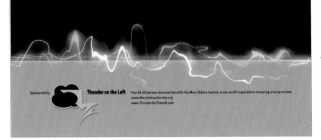

The graphic identity for a one-woman performance serves as both headline and logo. The headline uses a classic typeface that would look quite ordinary if not for the extremely compressed "O," and the small word "THE" tucked between letters.

Overlapping the headline on top of the images prevents the look of an ordinary layout that just stacks elements one above the other, plus it clearly unifies the disparate elements.

The images of the artist are single-frame video captures from mini-DV footage. I applied an "aged film" filter to the video before capturing the stills.

To find a graphic that would symbolize podcasting, I did a search for "wave form" at iStockPhoto.com.

I repeated the tan headline color in the body text and in the bottom imprint area to help tie all of the floating elements together as a single visual element.

In the small ad version, I placed the tan color over the image for visual consistency. This also helps to make the white text and headline/logo stand out.

This is a series of small space ad banners for a historically researched book about a 16th-century woman. The ads were designed for newspaper web sites at colleges and universities.

To relate to the target audience—students—the headline is presented as a final exam question and hints at the controversial premise of the book.

An oversized ornament is used as a visual device to grab attention and convey a sense of the time period examined in the book.

The dark-on-dark color scheme (yellow ochre ornament on a dark gray background) creates strong contrast with the white text.

The ads can easily be converted to black and white to run in campus newspapers.

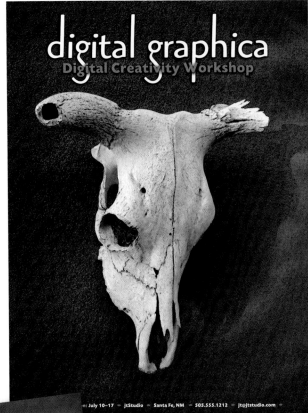

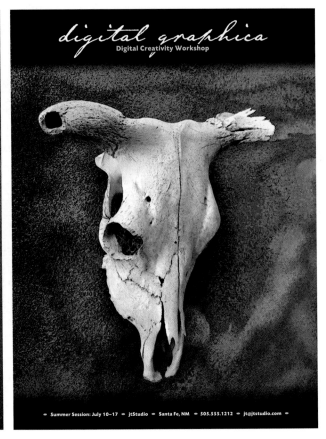

This is the original, mediocre photo before I modified it in Photoshop.

The promotional poster for a series of workshops about creative digital imagery combines simplicity with contrast—a formula for strong visual impact that almost always works. The typographic treatment in this version is interesting, but its size and unusual letterforms compete with the skull image, and the color of the tag line conflicts with the color in the poster.

In this version, the typography is less visually dominant. The black shading at the top and bottom create strong fields of contrast for the text. These blocks also visually organize the layout into disparate shapes that separate the event information from the event image. I brought out colors that were hidden in the skull image by using a technique of scrubbing in certain areas of various Photoshop Channels with the Dodge Tool. Strong visual impact is created by the unexpected coloration of the image, both skull and background. (Do you see the bird's nest in the eye socket?)

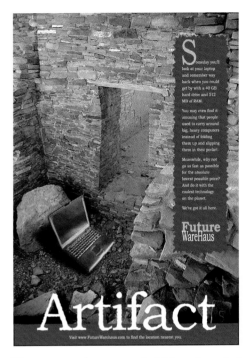

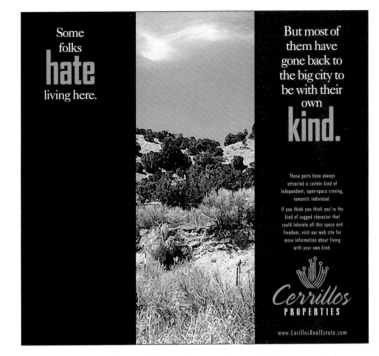

The conceptual contrast of a high-tech symbol in a setting of ancient ruins, combined with strong contast of values between the white headline and the rich color image, creates a memorable image and an ad that begs to be read. To maximize the impact of the photo, we made it as large as possible. Even though the text is lengthy (for an ad), the text and the logo visually combine as a single element with the background shape. The oversized capital "S" is just a playful, color graphic accent to balance the weight of the logo at the bottom of the text.

The one-word headline blasts off the page in bright white. We roughened the edges of its letterforms to add a little "ancient" personality. We also stopped the photo a little short of the bottom and added the dark blue strip to improve the legibility of both the headline and the small copy below it.

This magazine ad for a realtor grabs attention with its unusual three-panel design that separates an unexpected headline from the main visual and the rest of the text.

Instead of a uniformly large headline, we created a strong visual impact with the extreme contrast in font sizes and styles. We floated the first part of the headline at the top of the left-side vertical panel, which isolates it as a dramatic, attention-getting element. The emphasis on a controversial word attracts readers' eyes. By using the same emphasis in a word on the right-side panel (repetition), we made a strong visual connection between the two sides, with the eye-candy image sandwiched between the two thoughts.

Look around

Advertising surrounds us, as you are well aware. But often we are not aware, not consciously, of how advertising affects us. We don't even notice which ones we see and which ones we ignore. If you are in charge of creating advertising, you need to become painfully aware of what everyone else is doing with it, and keep track of what works and what doesn't—at least visually.

Designer Exercise: Every day, everywhere you go, cut out advertisements and take a good look at them. Collect black-and-white newspaper ads that are great, black-and-white glossy magazine ads, and color ads. Put into words exactly what makes each one stand out. Is it the headline copy that caught your eye? Did the headline typeface and arrangement catch your eye? Is there an interesting visual image that you noticed before you noticed what the text said? Is the layout unusual, provocative, or suprising?

Finding advertisements that don't work very well is just as educative. Why doesn't it work? Is it the typeface choice? Is the layout just too dull or too flashy (either way, your eye wants to run away from it). Are the elements scattered all over the piece with no conscious thought to arrangement, to grouping similar elements together? Is there unnecessary junk cluttering it up? How is the ad aligned—are there several centered elements, each centered over a different center line? Are there items stuck in corners? Is the white space disorganized, causing visual disruption? And what exactly is not "working"—does the ad get the message across to its intended market, even if it's not very attractive? Or is it losing the market because no one who *should* read it *will* read it because it doesn't reflect, for instance, the quality of the product they are trying to sell?

Don't just notice the ads that appeal to you personally. Perhaps there is an ad for a heavy metal band that you don't particularly care for—does the ad visually appeal to the market it's aiming at? Lots of commercials during football games go right over Robin's head, but John eats them up. To create effective advertising yourself, you must become very conscious of what everyone else is doing.

10. Billboards

AND OTHER LARGE THINGS

In many areas of the country, billboards are cheaper than you might think—check into it. There are two basic types of outdoor advertising billboards. You might choose one or the other, or both types, in your billboard campaign, depending on your project and how many billboards you plan to use.

The **poster panel** is printed in strips and pasted on at the billboard locations. The most common size is approximately 25 feet by 12 feet. Poster panels are most effective as high-frequency (like all over town or all over the country), short-term postings.

Bulletins are available in several forms. You can create a panel that will be transferred onto flexible material or adhesive vinyl and stretched onto the bulletin frame. The most common sizes for these are 48 x 14 feet, 60 x 20, and 36 x 10. Bulletins are usually longer-term than poster panels and can add high impact at key locations, often as a supplement to a poster campaign.

You might see either one as you're driving around town or out in the country. For specific details on creating billboards, call your local outdoor advertising company, or search the web for "billboard signage."

Avoid the outdoor brochure look

Advertisers often make the mistake of trying to put too much information on an outdoor board. Outdoor advertising can be very effective as long as you (or the client) don't try to turn it into a brochure with detailed information and too many messages.

The most effective outdoor designs combine simplicity with visual impact. The most important of these two features is simplicity. Remember, your audience is driving by at a high speed (unless you've paid a premium price for a billboard on a freeway that always has a traffic jam) and one or two glances is all you can hope for. No matter how badly you want to put a phone number on the board, don't do it. How often do you risk your life grabbing pen and paper to write down phone numbers from outdoor boards? Whenever we see a phone number tucked into a board design, we wonder if the incredible optimist was the designer or the client. This may sound like a silly premise, but we've actually failed at times to convince clients that having too much in a design makes the entire board unreadable, useless, and a waste of money.

This outdoor design contains some nice elements, but it also has one very common bad feature: more information than can be absorbed in the few seconds that it's visible.

The first thing we did was eliminate everything except the information that is absolutely essential and select a simple western icon that is instantly recognizable, even from a distance. This preliminary version is much better than an outdoor board with too much on it.

We changed the size of some of the type, and added dotted lines to tie the hat into the composition and link the words of the event name together. The dotted lines serve as a subtle decorative element that could pass for something like western saddle stitching. To add a touch of color, we put accents in the hat band.

Next, we changed the placement of some of the dotted lines and reduced the size of the date. This version is simple, and everything can be read at a glance.

Most outdoor bulletins allow for adding an "embellishment" for a reasonable extra fee. In this example, the embellishment is the cut-out of the hat that extends above the shape of the board. This technique adds a lot of visual impact due to the unusual shape of the board that catches the eye, and it allows us to make the visual larger.

Even though phone numbers usually don't work on outdoor boards, we'll add a web address if we can make it readable and if the address is memorable. If you have a simple, concise domain name, the URL can be a valuable element of your design. Now the board's message, in two words, effectively says, "For complete details and all the information you could possibly want including photographs and maps, updated daily, visit our web site."

If the budget allows us to add an embellishment, we've got a design that's certain to be seen and actually read.

If you burden your design with lots of unnecessary copy, you diminish its effectiveness and make it a visual mess. This is a brochure painted on an outdoor board. Let go of all the extraneous information.

To turn this piece into an effective outdoor board, we used the logo of this furniture store for a headline, while the illustration and layout provide the message that they're avant garde, designy, contemporary, and trendsetters. The slanted type is an unexpected element that helps attract a driver's eye.

This cleaner, simplified design adds elements of readability, sophistication, and style that far outweigh the perceived advantage of having lots of information on the board.

Visual impact outdoors

No other advertising medium allows you such stunning visual impact. The ability to make your message larger than life can provide an image and personality for your client that not only creates tremendous visual impact, but also high visibility, recognition, and recall.

This was the first concept for the board. We loved the tiger, but it wasn't quite powerful enough. By enlarging the tiger, as shown below, we have less of the tiger on the board itself, but viewers' minds actually fill in the rest of the body and claws. Thus we actually get more space than we paid for—we get all the imaginary space that the tiger's body inhabits. Free.

The colorful, dramatic image in this design takes advantage of the strong contrast with the massive black background. Enlarging the tiger so huge simplifies the image while at the same time making it bolder and more intimidating.

155

This concept combines simplicity, an unexpected image for a florist, and a strong contrast between the white background and the dead flowers. This combination definitely gets the potential viewer's attention.

The contrast of typefaces in the logo adds to the visual interest. The contrast between the reversed subhead in the strong horizontal strip against the rectangular shape of the image area makes the subhead stand out.

Humor always gets attention. It can be in the form of illustrative style or in the headline copy. Even if the client's product or service is dead-serious, humor can act as a contrast to deliver the client's message.

In this example, the undersized subhead commands attention because of its strong contrast in the horizontal strip at the bottom of the billboard. The dark background color of the main image areas sets a shady mood and allows the headline to blast off the board. The unique font adds to the visual interest that catches a reader's eye.

Simplicity and visual impact always work. The question alone is enough to get people het up, so would you really need a graphic?

The Museum of Digital Art is having a show of digital cartoon art, as reflected in this poster design. The visual impact of the tightly cropped image emphasizes the stylized technique of the artists on display.

Like the billboard with the tiger, the viewer sees the rest of the face and head, thus expanding the visual presence beyond what we paid for.

Teen Help Line
555.1745
Talk it out with teens who've been there.

In the beginning of this chapter we recommended that you not waste your time putting phone numbers on outdoor boards, but you know the rule about rules. With creativity, you can make it work.

The color scheme of this outdoor campaign is designed to visually break the numbers into verbal words in your mind.

Teen Help Line
five, five, five seventeen forty-five

Another board in this outdoor campaign continues to feature the phone number, but this time verbally rather than numerically. The over-the-edge simplistic layout ensures that this board will be noticed.

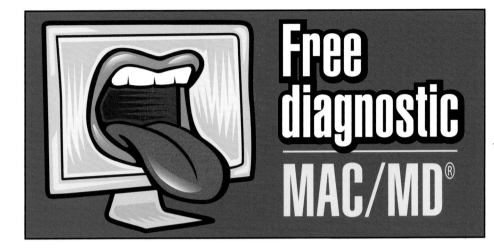

A simple visual pun combined with the simplest, most basic copy creates instant communication in the frantic, drive-by advertising world.

The background color blend adds visual interest to capture a driver's attention while also providing a strong contrast on the right side for the headline and logo.

Bold type, simplicity, and the unexpected, upside-down image make this outdoor design eye-catching and entertaining. Breaking the background into two colors adds visual interest and more color. It also solves the dilemma of the planet logo partially disappearing, as it would have against the black background. Solving problem details like this often leads to design solutions that might not have occurred to you had there not been a problem in the process.

Look around

If you live in or near a large city, you'll see lots of good examples of posters and painted bulletins on outdoor boards. Smaller cities may not have as many painted bulletins, but you can still find great examples and inspiration in the design books and design award annuals.

Designer Exercise: Be conscious every time you look at a billboard. You, as a driver, are the best critic. Are your eyes attracted to it? Can you read it? Do you understand the message? Is there extraneous stuff that just clutters the board? Is it clear what the billboard is trying to sell you? If there are directions to a place, can you follow the directions without having to write them down? Even if you don't have plans to create a billboard in the near future, train your mind to become aware of what works and what doesn't so you'll be ready when you do need to design one.

11. Web sites

A professional web site requires various disciplines, skills, and talents. While traditional design skills are important, it's equally important to acquire a comprehensive understanding of the technical aspects of web design. It's not necessary to become a full-fledged programmer, but a solid understanding of HTML and CSS (Cascading Style Sheets) code is essential because design decisions are often made in response to the limitations and challenges of web technology. That technology includes the various languages (code) that are used for web page appearance and functionality and the many different web browsers available to users that often interpret this code incorrectly.

Of course, the entire World Wide Web is one huge portfolio of web site design. As you browse from site to site, pay special attention to how they're designed. You'll probably notice that most current sites are using layouts that are typical of CSS design: content constrained to a fixed width container, multiple-column layouts that contain both stretching and non-stretching columns, CSS styled navigation links and buttons instead of graphics, page elements that have fixed positions on the page, backgrounds that remain fixed when the rest of the page content scrolls, etc.

This chapter is several thousand pages too short to give technical details of how to actually build web sites. However, in addition to the examples shown, we've arranged for several million examples to be available on the World Wide Web. ;)

The basics

There are many visual and technical things to consider when designing a web site. A short list of important considerations includes:

Appreciate code and what it can do

Web *design* (the visual aspect) and web *development* (the technical aspect) are interconnected and influence each other constantly throughout the process. The more technical knowledge you have, the better web designer you'll be. Your designs will function better and they'll be easier to build.

Learn as much about development as possible, even if you plan to only *design* web sites and have someone else *build* them. Understanding the structures and limitations of web site design helps to ensure that your great design ideas are realized as you envisioned them—and not modified by a developer whose sense of design doesn't match your expectations.

Be clear about the purpose of the site

Create a design that lets users know immediately what the site offers—information, products, services, etc.

Make speed a priority

Don't make users wait long periods of time for Flash files to load. Flash navigation and animation can be a very good thing—as long as they don't test the patience of the user.

Remember basic design principles

Create page layouts that have strong and clear content organization based on contrast, alignment, repetition, and proximity. Make the most important information the most visible.

Use restraint in color schemes. Limited use of color can be more seductive and pleasing than a visual assault of rainbow colors blasting off the page.

Apply basic "User Interface" guidelines

Aim for simplicity and consistency. All pages in a site should have a consistent look and the navigation should be intuitive (easy to figure out), familiar (use the same navigation system throughout the site), and forgiving (always provide an easy path from any page to any other page).

Pamper your typography

When you create *graphics* that include typography, apply the same typographic standards you would in print. Bad letter-spacing and dumb quotations marks may be unavoidable in HTML text, but it's inexcusable in graphic text.

Make text a readable size

Super-small text is really cool-looking and it provides lots of nice design space on a page. It's also very irritating if you don't have perfect vision. Most sites can be set up so the visitor can enlarge the text on a page, but the extremely small text appears most often in Flash sites where it can't be enlarged. Make user-friendly design a priority.

Proofread and test your site

It's almost a certainty that your site contains typos or grammatical errors. Get several people to proofread it for you. Test your site in the most common versions of the most popular browsers on Mac, Linux, and Windows computers.

Don't be annoying

Don't use non-stop, nerve-rattling animations that interfere with readability or patience. Subtle Flash animation can contribute to a page when used wisely.

Horizontal rules and tables with embossed borders turned on are turn-offs. Very 1990s stuff.

Don't use hokey animations that you downloaded for free, such as rainbows and letters flying into little mailboxes.

CSS design

Web technology is constantly changing. We used to create pages by designing a graphic in Photoshop, slicing it apart, then putting the slices into cells of tables on a web page. The tables held the graphic pieces together and in position. Some table cells were used to hold text or graphics and some held tiny, invisible spacer graphics that kept empty table cells from collapsing and ruining the layout.

This technique still works, but there's a better way called **CSS (Cascading Style Sheets).** CSS code can describe the appearance and positioning of every element of a page's design in an external style sheet (the style sheet can also be embedded in the web page's HTML file). The HTML file that contains all of the page's content refers to the external CSS file.

The goal of CSS design is to separate page content from page design and appearance. CSS style sheets enable you to easily and quickly make style changes to an entire site.

To illustrate this concept, visit **cssZenGarden.com** (shown below). The appearance of the Zen Garden page is controlled by an external CSS style sheet. To change the page's appearance, users can click on one of the style names in a list of styles. The content (the text) on the page remains the same, but the layout and design changes dramatically. In the HTML file for the page, each section or element of the page has a property name. An external CSS style sheet includes instructions for the appearance and positioning (and sometimes the behavior) of each element on the page. Depending on the style sheet you select, the page looks completely different because the instructions in each style sheet are different.

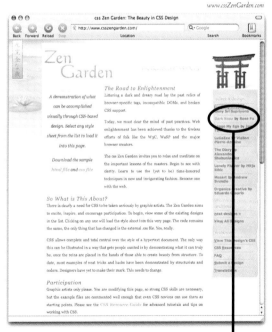

The CSS Zen Garden site includes a list of style sheets. Click a style sheet name to apply that style sheet to the current page.

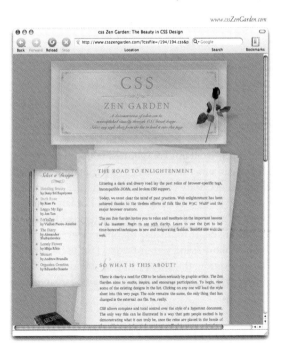

The "Dark Rose" style sheet has been applied to the page for a completely different appearance. The content is unchanged.

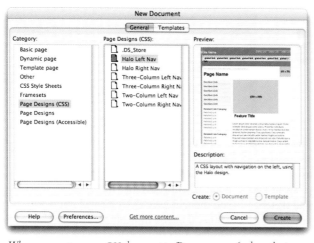

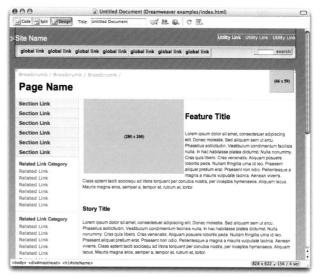

When you create a new CSS document in Dreamweaver (web-authoring software from Adobe), you can choose from several CSS layout templates. In the "New Document" window above, we chose a category of "Page Designs (CSS)," then the "Halo Left Nav" template (shown to the right).

The "Halo Left Nav" template can be modified with custom text and images. You can delete existing elements, add additional items, and modify the colors. If you prefer to start with a blank page, you can create a new HTML document, then add CSS elements as shown below.

Create a layout

There are many ways to create a layout for your web site. If you need to show a design layout to a client, or if you just want to experiment with page design, the most common technique is to create a layout in Photoshop.

When your design comps are ready to show, it's easy to save the designs as JPEGs and email them to the client. Or upload them to a web site where the client can see them.

As shown in the examples on this page, web-authoring software (such as Dreamweaver, shown here) provides templates and visual aids for creating different styles of CSS pages.

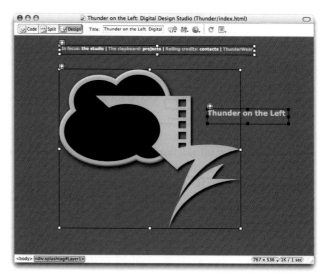

Dreamweaver lets you place text and images in containers called "Layers" that you can drag to any position on the page. Dreamweaver automatically writes the CSS code that describes each layer's position, plus text attributes such as font, color, and size. This type of site is a combination of traditional HTML and CSS and is referred to as "transitional."

Web page specifications

Standard web page graphics should use a resolution of 72 ppi (pixels per inch). The color mode should always be RGB (Red, Green, Blue).

Page size for a web site is a tricky subject. We all have differently sized monitors with different screen resolution settings. Some people have their browser window open to a full-screen and some like their browser window smaller. This means the presentation of your web site will look slightly different on all these different computers. There's no perfect solution for this issue, so most designers compromise with a page size that works for the majority of viewers.

A page size that fits the most common monitors is 800 pixels wide by 600 pixels tall. The 800 pixels includes 25 pixels for the scroll bar on the right side of the browser, so you should keep any important content within a 775 pixel width.

Locate the site navigation so it's always visible when the page opens—never make users scroll to find the navigation! We prefer that the *initial visual impression* of the home page be contained in the 800 x 600 window, while the depth of other pages is of course more flexible.

www.BazzaniCouture.com | designed by AgilityGraphics.com

Now the site has been optimized for 800 by 600 pixels. It fits perfectly in a browser open to that size.

These examples show what happens when a site designed for 1024 x 768 pixels (top) is opened in a standard browser window size of 800 x 600 (bottom). The navigation elements disappear due to their placement.

This secondary page has vertical CSS navigation on the left, simple and clean.

This site uses horizontal CSS navigation across the top of the page. The subtle animations in this Flash site combine with a modernistic graphic look to create an ambience of technical expertise and creative abilities.

Navigation systems

Navigation is the way in which visitors interact with the web site and get to where they want to go. It's the connection between the viewer and the web site. Its ease of use is essential for the success of the site. If your navigation doesn't work correctly, if it's unclear or complicated, no one will get to your nicely designed secondary pages.

It's important that the navigation is visible and intuitive right from the start. The user should immediately understand how to use it, so make it easy for them. Endless nested drop-down and fly-out menus or complicated twitchy Flash navigations make life difficult for the user. Flash and CSS fly-out menus can be effective if done with a degree of subtlety and sophistication.

The look of your navigation system is usually influenced by your target audience, but generally you can ask yourself the following questions about its effectiveness: Is it clear at first glance where to find everything? Are buttons clearly recognizable as buttons (or links)? Will a less experienced user be able to navigate the site easily?

The navigation system should provide a button or link for every section of the site on every page (notice we said every *section*, not every *page*). To test your navigation, ask someone who's not familiar with your project to browse through your site and give you feedback about how easy or hard it is. Their comments will tell you what works and what doesn't.

In most cases, don't invent new concepts of navigation that have never been seen before. Strive for navigation design that's intuitive, friendly, and familiar.

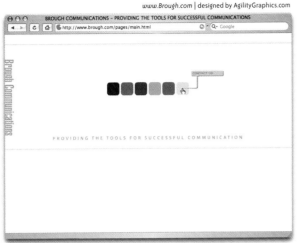

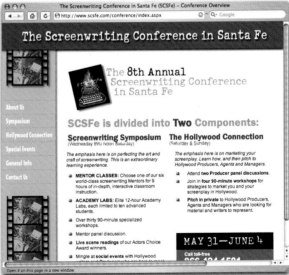

The navigation in this Flash site's minimalist design approach provides pop-up captions when the mouse hovers over the color shapes. The aim is to create a sense of sophisticated design and creative problem solving.

The navigation on secondary pages is similar (repetitive and familiar), but adds a variation: when the mouse hovers over a colored nav shape, a caption appears to the right of the navigation.

The navigation of this site is on the left, but it's crowded, dark, and somber-looking. The colors used for emphasis in the navigation area are unappealing, and the overall visual impression is not as elegant as it could be.

A redesign of the page simplifies the navigation and leaves sub-categories to be revealed with fly-out menus. The color scheme is changed and some text blurbs are moved to prevent crowding the main event graphic at the top.

No design is sometimes better than bad design. Which of the layouts above would you rather read? Which one looks more professional?

Text considerations

The line length of copy on web pages affects its readability. Very long lines of text are hard to read because it's difficult to keep track of which line is the next one down when your eye jumps back to the left. Shorter line lengths make reading online easier.

Strong contrast between text and the background color is essential. Reading text that has a similar value as its background, such as red type on a blue background, is tedious and tiring.

Don't crowd text when it appears within a shape; if your text is inside a shape (such as a box), add some padding so the text has breathing room. Don't crowd text with graphics. Extra space around text always makes it more inviting and easier to read.

Type that overlays textured or patterned backgrounds is hard to read. Sometimes impossible. Aim for maximum readability—good contrast and a simple background.

In the example below, we used harmonious colors, but there's still enough contrast for excellent readability.

CSS web sites

CSS is a coding language used to format HTML documents, as explained and shown on pages 163–164. The extent to which you use CSS will vary based on your skill level, but it has become the standard and recommended way to build web sites. CSS design makes HTML code more efficient, easier to read, faster to load, and easier to update.

Validate CSS pages

If you use CSS, you can "validate" your pages to ensure that you used proper code and that your pages will display correctly. To validate CSS pages, go to **http://jigsaw. w3.org/css-validator**. Enter your site's URL and click "Check." A web page is returned with validation information. Click the "valid HTML" link (circled to the right) to see specific problems in your code.

The validation page that opens (shown below, right) lists specific coding problems found on the submitted page and provides information about how to correct them.

There are plenty of occasions when it's necessary to use traditional tables in your page layout. For instance, when you need to organize large amounts of information in a tabular fashion, an HTML table is the easiest way to do it. If you're not comfortable using pure CSS to create table-like content organization, you can create a traditional HTML table and place it within a div tag—the CSS element that Dreamweaver calls a "Layer."

Whether you use CSS or tables for the layout of your pages, you should always use CSS to format text—size, color, line spacing, etc.—because CSS style sheets offer so much more control over the appearance of text. If you create the style sheet as an *external* style sheet (instead of an *internal* style sheet that's embedded in the code of a single page), any or all of your HTML pages can point to it. When you make changes in the style sheet, the change is instantly applied to *all* HTML pages that use that style sheet.

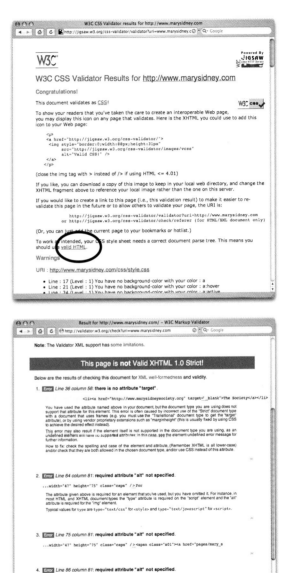

The example above shows a page constructed with CSS that includes traditional HTML tables. In the page code, the tables are placed within CSS div tags that define their position on the page, as well as other properties, such as the padding around the tables that separates them from the surrounding borders and page graphics.

The Mondrian-style layout for ShimaStyle.com echoes the look and style of the bags featured, while providing a sophisticated, contemporary layout grid. The decision to use grays as background colors allows the product colors to dominate the page and act as the focal points of the layout.

This site is about the research surrounding a 16th-century woman. The graphics and typography give a sense of the time period, while the well-organized layout presents information in an uncluttered presentation.

Flash sites

www.BillWallLeather.com | *designed by DNA Communications*

In the hands of an experienced Flash designer, Flash animation and technology can create an entertaining viewing experience that communicates your message clearly and in a compelling way.

While a lot of developers still build the classic Flash site with in-and-out animations to each page/section, an intro, and lots of little moving parts, there is a trend to minimize that whole aspect and to build Flash sites that are more to the point and focused on the content.

The benefit of this use of Flash is that it allows greater control over the design of your pages, while being as fast and easy to view as HTML pages. You can control how and in what order things are loaded, introduced, and dealt with. You can provide the viewer with a more cohesive experience; each section can seamlessly transform into the next by loading Flash files into other Flash files, rather than having each section's file embedded on a different HTML page.

One aspect to consider when designing entirely Flash sites is that the capability of search engines to point to specific content is limited. Meta-crawlers that index pages for search engines can't read links on Flash pages or the content inside of Flash files.

This visually rich site contains enough Flash animation to entertain viewers without becoming tiresome.

The navigation links light up and move slightly when moused over. The jewelry in the main image glitters and sparkles. When a photo is clicked, it blurs, then opens in its own window.

When someone mentions full Flash sites, most people think of slow preloading and long animations that you have to sit through each time you visit a site. These stereotypes may have been true in the past, but Flash has matured far beyond that. You might have even seen Flash sites without being aware they used Flash files. While Flash technology is known for intricate animations, video streaming, and 3D rendering, it has also become a superb tool for creating interactive pages that enhance communication and deliver a message in a unique and memorable way.

www.RothRitter.com | designed by Roth Ritter at DNA Communications

www.DNAcommunications.com | designed by DNA Communications

Elegant design and subtle animation in the graphics and navigation informs the visitor immediately that this is a high-end design firm. The mention of high-profile clients on the home page also helps.

This stunning and fascinating site is for a web designer whose hobby is astrophotography. The intro page contains a center section of animated nebulae and galaxies. The non-obtrusive animation adds beauty and mystery, compelling visitors to enter. Interior pages are beautifully styled CSS pages without Flash animation.

www.KenKaySF.com | designed by LStudio.net

The KenKay Associates site features elegant dissolves of the main images when new pages load. The similar visual structure and organization of each page makes the entire site easy to read and navigate.

www.CMSCKids.org | designed by DNA Communications

Flash adds fun and whimsy as elements tumble onto the page in this site designed for children. One section provides a magnifying glass for kids to drag around the screen.

Database-driven sites and CMS

Database-driven web sites interact with the information in a database that's stored on a server. The database can be kept up-to-date and current by as many people as necessary. Database sites display specific information when called upon, rather than having all the information placed on individual, static pages. These sites can gather or save information from or to a database, then display that information on a page when a user requests it. Database-driven sites make up a huge part of the Internet today. This type of site can actually create web pages dynamically (on the fly), using the latest information stored in the database.

You've experienced this kind of site, even if you weren't aware of it. Amazon, eBay, and your online bank are just a few examples.

Generally, databases are integrated into web sites when feedback is needed right away or when the amount of information required on the site is beyond what humans can handle manually. Or, if your site contains information that must be updated frequently, a database solution can keep information updated automatically. Whenever large amounts of information need to be stored and later displayed on a page, database integration is the best solution.

mySQL is a free "open source" database program available for download on the Internet. Both Flash and HTML/CSS pages can interact with it. It's easy to find mySQL tutorials, information, and user forums on the Internet to help you learn about it.

www.SCSFe.com | designed by DenimTech.com

This conference site is large and has information that changes often. The original site was redesigned using database integration and CMS. This enables various conference staff members to update the site through a browser on any computer. Conference directors have individual passwords that give them private access to sensitive information compiled by the database, such as credit card information for online payments and financial spreadsheet information for the event.

Site produced by Landonsea design.
Art direction, design and Flash by Landon Dowlen.
CSS programming and custom CMS by Chris Gordon.

CMS stands for **Content Management System,** which has become very popular in web development. A CMS provides an easy way for non-technical content providers to add or edit content without knowing anything about HTML or web design. Anyone who has permission to open the CMS template can make changes to specified areas. The site administrator determines who can access certain areas of a page and what kind of changes can be made (text only, or text and images).

To set up a content management system, you will need to work with a programmer. Or check out software called **Contribute** from Adobe. It works with Dreamweaver software to create web page templates that can be edited online from any browser on any computer. Someone with the proper access permission can open the page template and change the content of designated sections of the page. The site administrator (or site designer) designates what parts of the page can be edited.

Staffers responsible for maintaining this site go to the Site Administration page and sign in. They choose the section they want to edit or update.

An editable area is provided for changing that page's text.

Template-based design

Web design today requires more familiarity with coding and programming than ever before. A growing number of web sites offer a solution that provides less experienced designers with pre-designed web sites that can be edited and modified. Some site templates are free, others are for sale, ranging from around $30 to $1,200 and more. Search the web for "CSS templates."

Working with a template and adapting it to your own project is a good way to learn more about CSS design. Templates often include graphics, the original layered Photoshop file for making modifications, and even complete Flash animations.

For a start, visit 4Templates.com or TheTemplateStore.com. There are many sites that offer free templates, advice, and instructions about how to implement various features.

Two of the best sites for learning more about CSS are cssZenGarden.com and aListApart.com.

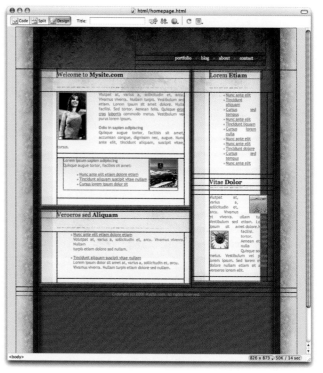

This template was purchased from 4Templates.com for $30. It can be customized to fit your own project. Along with the HTML files, you get the original layered Photoshop files, Flash and non-Flash versions of the site if the template has Flash components, the CSS style sheet file, and a collection of TrueType fonts used in the templates found at this site. Just customizing a template can be a frustrating experience, but it's also another way to learn how web sites are constructed.

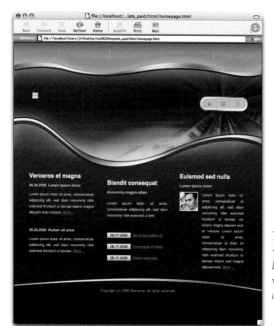

This is another template from 4Templates.com. You can open the layered Photoshop file that's included with the web files and add your company logo to the red area.

178

12. Tables of Contents & Indices

Most people don't think too much about tables of contents. But there are those among us who love them. There are so many ways to be creative, but it really helps to know your software so you can implement your creative ideas easily.

Tables of contents

Tables of contents (TOCs) are designed very differently for books, magazines, newsletters, and other publications. When you bump up against one of these projects, be sure to look around and see what others are doing, what works, and what doesn't. Always, though, you'll find that the same basic rules apply: contrast, repetition, alignment, and proximity.

Leaders

One of the key features of a table of contents is usually the leaders, the dots that lead to the page numbers. Below are several examples of the variations you can play with in leaders.

Examples of leaders:

✳ ✳ ✳ ✳ ✳ ✳ ✳ ✳ ✳ ✳ ✳ ✳ ✳ ✳ ✳ ✳

)()()()()()()()()()()()()()()()( )

> >

•‥•‥•‥•‥•‥•‥•‥•‥•‥•‥•‥•‥•

123456781234567812345678123456781234567812345678123456781234 5

⋯⋯⋯⋯⋯⋯⋯⋯⋯⋯⋯⋯⋯⋯⋯⋯⋯⋯

‥‥‥ ‥‥‥ ‥‥‥ ‥‥‥ ‥‥‥ ‥‥‥

▯ ▯ ▯ ▯ ▯ ▯ ▯ ▯ ▯ ▯ ▯ ▯ ▯ ▯ ▯ ▯ ▯ ▯ ▯

▯•▯•▯•▯•▯•▯•▯•▯•▯•▯•▯•▯•▯

:::

🐪 🐪 🐪 🐪 🐪 🐪 🐪 🐪 🐪 🐪 🐪 🐪 🐪 🐪 🐪 🐪 🐪

🐪 🐪 🐪 🐪 🐪 🐪 🐪 🐪 🐪 🐪 🐪

Don'ts

There are several basic things to be careful of when designing the table of contents, as illustrated on these two pages.

> › **Don't** create leaders that don't match, as shown at the top-right. Sometimes a contrast of leaders can be a design feature, but make sure there is *enough* contrast between the different leaders that it is *obviously* a design decision and not just that you didn't know any better.

The leaders in the first level don't match the leaders in the second level, but they are similar. "Similar" causes conflict. A reader might wonder if it's perhaps a mistake.

In this example, the leaders were customized so they are identical.

If the leaders don't match, then make it very clear they don't match. Use it as a design feature.

> **Don't** create leaders by typing periods over and over again! They will never line up properly, as you can see above. Every program that allows you to set text has some feature for adding leaders automatically. Learn to use your software!

> **Don't** set the page numbers far away from the content, even if there are leaders.

> **Don't** separate related items; remember the principle of proximity. In the example above, the first level heads have the same amount of space above them as below, but the first level heads really need to be *closer* to the second level heads *below* them, since that is what they are identifying. Close the gap.

> **Don't** confuse the various levels, as in the example above-left. Make the levels different enough that a reader can instantly tell which is which, as in the example above-right. Use the principles of contrast (make certain elements very different), proximity (group the head with its subheadings), and repetition (repeat the groupings and the alignments so the reader understands the organization).

Possibilities

On these pages are a few possibilities of type treatments for a table of contents. It's a fun challenge to make the contents both beautiful and functional!

Designing with type

The page numbers in this example are set one point size smaller than the type. The leaders were reduced in point size (every program lets you customize the leaders). This particular leader actually consists of three characters: period space space. Using the spaces prevents the dots from being crammed too close together. Check your software and see how many different characters you can set for leaders.

The Internet and the World Wide Web

You are, of course, using style sheets, yes? If not, you should—they are one of the most important features to learn in your page layout or word processing software. Using style sheets, set up a definition for a first level, second level, and third level if necessary, as well as section headers and chapter numbers (if the chapter numbers are set separately from the contents, as shown above and left). Then after the table of contents is on the page, you can fine-tune it with the click of a button—add a wee bit more space above each first level chapter heading, move the page numbers to the left a bit more, add more space between the leader dots, see what all the second levels look like with a different font, etc.

If you have different sections in your table of contents, use the typography and design to make it very clear to the reader the difference between a section and a chapter.

Notice how the four basic elements of design even show up in a table of contents: contrast, repetition, alignment, and proximity.

By the way, capitalize the TOC entries to match the capitalization used in the chapters.

In this example, the chapter numbers pick up the same font as the section headings so you can differentiate between the chapter numbers on the left and the page numbers on the right.

Above, the page numbers for the section headings and the chapters (both on the right side) are the same; if your software sets different fonts for the different levels, use your program's search-and-replace feature to make them all consistent.

Because there are so many numbers in a table of contents, it's nice to use an expert set that includes oldstyle figures, as shown in the column to the right. But many oldstyle figures do not line up in columns, as you can see. This sometimes makes the leaders misalign as well. The simple solution is to set a right-aligned leader tab where you want the dots (or dashes or whatever) to end, then another right-aligned tab for the numbers. Or use an OpenType font that includes "tabular oldstyle" numbers so they'll automatically align.

So in each line above, there are four tabs: a right-aligned tab to the chapter number, a left-aligned tab to the chapter title, a right-aligned tab to the end of the leaders, and a right-aligned tab for the page numbers.

If the numbers are close enough to their titles, sometimes you don't even need leaders at all.

35	**Barbara Sikora**
41	**Ronnie Madrid**
47	**Barbara Riley**
53	**Harrah Lord**
87	**Amy Meilander**
93	**Laura Taylor**
101	**Jeanne Bahnson**
113	**Carmen Sheldon**
121	**Kathy Thornley**

The page number doesn't always have to come *after* the title (as also shown in the section headings to the left). Just make sure the ones are in the ones column, the tens are in the tens column, and the hundreds are in the hundreds column (set a right-aligned tab for the numbers, then hit a tab *before* you type the number).

If you center your table of contents, please remember the principle of proximity: related items belong together. If the page number is the same distance below one title heading as it is above the other (as often happens), it makes it very difficult to tell which page the chapter begins upon.

In this centered example, it is clear that the page number belongs to the title it follows.

As usual when centering lines of text, watch where the lines break. For instance, don't do something like this:

WHY THERE IS AN AUTHORSHIP
QUESTION

Instead, break the line at a logical place:

WHY THERE IS
AN AUTHORSHIP QUESTION

c o n t e n t s

Tables of contents don't have to be stuffy, of course. They should, however, reflect the content of the project. This example above is for a book that celebrates lawless typography, ugly typefaces, and layouts that break the rules.

Contents

Even though we call this a "table of contents," the heading for this page is generally just labeled "contents."

If your chapters or sections have various subcategories, use typography to differentiate between the various sections. If you're not printing in color, you can still take advantage of gray type to help categorize. The example above uses a script face for the Contents head, section titles, and chapter numbers (Shelley Volante) for contrast and repetition; a sans serif (ITC Officina Sans Black) in various tints of black as section identifiers, chapter heads, and subheads; a classic oldstyle serif (Adobe Caslon Pro) for headings within chapters, and the oldstyle proportional numbers for the pages.

186

INSIDE THIS ISSUE

Inside this issue

Inside this issue

The table of contents in a newsletter obviously isn't as lengthy as in a book, but there's no reason not to put some design thought into it. The example above is the sort of table that often appears in newsletters. It won't take much to make it look nicer.

Avoid putting the contents (or anything) into a box that crowds the text. Avoid the standard gray background. Although the example above-left looks significantly different from the examples to the right, only minor changes were actually made. For instance, directly to the right:

> Instead of a solid border, we made a very thin border with a thick top bar for **contrast** and another black bar at the bottom for **repetition** to tie the box together.

> Instead of the title centered in all caps, we reversed it out of the black bar and **aligned** it with the list of contents.

> We moved the columns of numbers into closer **proximity** with the list so they would be easier to read.

> We chose a different typeface (although it is exactly the same type size as the original).

Of course, this is a **repetition** of the typeface we are using elsewhere in the newsletter.

> We opened up the leaders a bit so they wouldn't create such a crowded line.

> We took out a little bit of the space between each line so it would make a more compact unit.

> In the top example, we used a tint of a color instead of the gray, and we took the border off. The color, of course, is one that we use in the rest of the newsletter.

FEATURE ARTICLES

5 WAY OF THE ARTIST: THE WORK OF ARI
*Discover the brilliant, lost work of this
amazing tenth-century Turkish artist.*

13 WRITING THE NEW FILM NOIR
*Alienation, desperation, smoky seedy bars,
wet streets at night, unsympathetic characters.*

16 TINSELTOWN ON THE INTERNET
*Avoiding script-reader hell can turn into
a soap opera.*

20 MINDS ABOVE THE MUSIC
*Summer music from blues to opera,
in the theater or on the farm.*

Feature Articles

WAY OF THE ARTIST: THE WORK OF ARI **| 5**
*Discover the brilliant, lost work of this
amazing tenth-century Turkish artist.*

WRITING THE NEW FILM NOIR **| 13**
*Alienation, desperation, smoky seedy bars,
wet streets at night, unsympathetic characters.*

TINSELTOWN ON THE INTERNET **| 16**
*Avoiding script-reader hell can turn
into a soap opera.*

MINDS ABOVE THE MUSIC **| 20**
*Summer music from blues to opera,
in the theater or on the farm.*

› These are just a few design
ideas for a small table of
contents as in a newsletter or
a book that doesn't contain
many chapters (or colors).

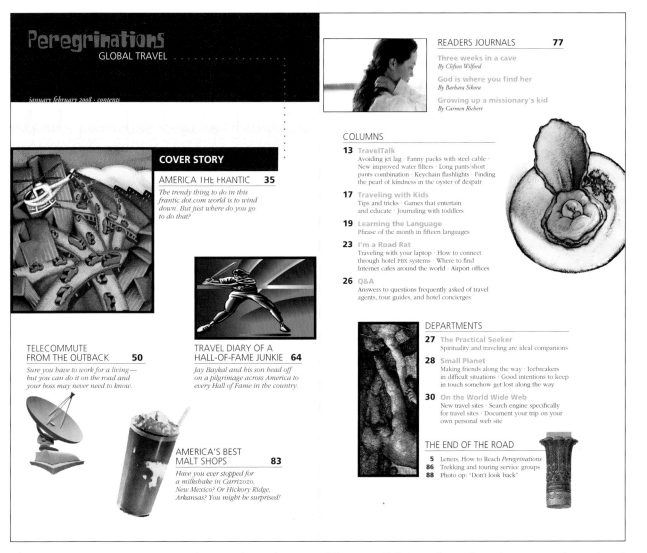

Peregrinations
GLOBAL TRAVEL

january february 2008 · contents

The contents pages in magazines are the most fun to design because they are usually in full color and, depending on the magazine of course, can often be quite playful. We're only showing you one example here because each layout is dependent on the magazine—its look-and-feel, its tone, and its message.

The same ol' design rules apply, and you can easily see them in this example: contrast, repetition, alignment, and proximity. If you get an opportunity to design one of these, you're probably already a pretty good designer. Go to a magazine rack and study the wonderful variety of options to get some ideas.

Indexes

An index is one of the most important parts of a book or lengthy publication, but it is amazing how often the typography in an index conspires to make it difficult to use. Just as in tables of contents, you really must know your style sheet feature in your software to format an index.

The most important design element in relation to indices is contrast. The reader should be able to scan the index and, because of typographic contrast, instantly know whether an entry is at the first level or the second level. A reader should not have to turn back a page to see if the entries at the top of the left-hand page are first or second level, as shown in the example to the right. With that said, there are endless variations of contrast to make an index not only attractive to look at, but useful for the reader.

Let's say you opened a manual to this page in the index (which is a real example from a manual I won't name). Would you know whether the items in the column are first levels or second levels? Even the header (next to the page number, upper-left) doesn't give you a clue—it tells you it's the "INDEX" (duh) instead of providing the first first-level entry on the page.

Also, what's with all the space between enries? It makes it difficult for the user to scan the items and looks as if it's an attempt to make the index appear to have more content than it really does.

alid photo ID required for all returns, (except for credit card purchases) xchanges and to receive and redeem store credit. With a receipt, a full fund in the original form of payment will be issued for new and unread oks and unopened music within 30 days from any Barnes & Noble store. merchandise purchased with a check, a store credit will be issued within first seven days. Without an original receipt, a store credit will be issued he lowest selling price. With a receipt, returns of new and unread books unopened music from bn.com can be made for store credit. ooks after 14 days or without a receipt are not returnable. Used books ot returnable.

A strong contrast of fonts between the first- and second-level heads lets the reader skim the index easily. It is instantly clear exactly which entries are first level and which ones are second level, even if you turn to a new page and the first column carries over from the previous page. Don't the oldstyle numbers in this version look so much nicer than the lining numbers in the original version?

Notice the index on the opposite page doesn't use commas between the entries and the page numbers. That is one optional style, but we prefer to use the comma because there are times when a lack of a comma can create confusion, as in this entry:

Windows 98 212

Is information about Windows on pages 98 and 212? Or is information about Windows 98 on page 212?

◄ *On the left is a typical index. It's neat and clean, but a reader has to look very closely to discern between first level entries and second level entries.*

On the right are exactly ► *the same two columns, but the first-level entries have more contrast. Anywhere readers open the index, they instantly understand the hierarchy of information.*

Now, at a glance you might think this index looks just fine. But if you look closely, you see there are quotation marks around some items and others start with periods (circled); those marks make the entries appear to be indented, which can confuse the reader. We need to hang the marks into the margins (as shown on the opposite page).

Also, the bold page numbers in the first-level entries call too much attention to themselves. We'll make all the page numbers match throughout the index, using the software's search-and-replace feature.

◀ Notice the quotation marks and periods have been hung into the margins, making the alignment neat and clean. (If you don't know how to hang punctuation, see *The Non-Designer's Type Book.*)

The numbers all match, and they are all oldstyle figures. Compare these to the first example on the opposite page—don't the lining figures in that first example look rather horsey compared to these oldstyle numbers?

Also notice how much nicer and less obnoxious are the acronyms in small caps in the final version as compared to the acronyms in all caps in the original version.

If you look carefully under the first-level entry "patterns" in that first example you see the phrase "Windows 98" has separated into two lines, which is confusing. To prevent this from happening, use a non-breaking space between the words instead of the regular Spacebar space (check the manual for your particular application).

Look around

You probably won't be interested in looking at tables of contents or indices critically until you have to design or lay out one yourself. But becoming conscious of the interesting variety of ways these seemingly mundane projects can be approached increases your design creativity in all areas.

Designer Exercise: Be conscious of the layout and design of every table of contents in every magazine, book, and newsletter you come across. Notice how different elements are aligned, what kinds of typefaces are used, how contrast is used within the type and the layout to facilitate finding the important information, and how items are grouped together. Look at the layouts of magazine tables of contents and the images that may be integrated with it; notice the croppings on the photos or illustrations; notice how the images are tied with the text; notice the alignments and the repetition of type and contrast.

Whenever possible, make copies of tables of contents and indices and make notes on them. Even more than many other design projects, these in particular must be functional as well as beautiful. It might make a lovely page to have lots of linespace between all the entries in an index, but doesn't all that excess space make it more difficult for a reader to scan? As with all the other projects in this book, knowing what makes a table of contents or index fail is just as important as knowing what makes it successful.

13. Newsletters & Brochures

Newsletters and brochures both involve the challenge of working with a lot of text and somehow seamlessly integrating the images into the text. It's interesting to us to see how some designers love and prefer working with lots of copy and others prefer working with minimal copy but lots of imagery. No matter what your preference, though, you'll probably end up doing a newsletter or two in your life.

Lots of text

The goal of a newsletter or brochure is to encourage people to actually read it. Large amounts of text make our eyes glaze over, so it's the designer's job to attract a reader's eye into the piece where hopefully they will find an article that interests them. Even if an article doesn't really interest certain readers, you can entice them into reading little chunks, which leads to other little chunks, and eventually they read the entire piece.

VIOLATE HUSKINGS
Ore ornery aboard inner gelded ketch. Aye rheumatic starry.
DARN HONOR FORM
Heresy rheumatic starry offer former's dodder. Violate Huskings, an wart hoppings darn honor form.

Violate lift wetter fodder, oiled Former Huskings, hoe hatter repetition fur bang furry retch—an furry stenchy. Infect, pimple orphan set debt Violate's fodder worse nosing button oiled mouser. Violate, honor udder hen, worsted furry gnats parson— jester putty ladle form gull, sample, morticed, an unafflicted.

Wan moaning Former Huskings nudist haze dodder setting honor cheer, during nosing. *Violate!* shorted dole former, watcher setting darn fur. Denture nor yore canned gat retch setting darn during nosing. Germ pup otter debt cheer.

Arm tarred, fodder, resplendent Violate warily.

Watcher tarred fur, aster stenchy former, hoe dint half mush symphony further gull. Are badger dint doe mush woke disk moaning. Ditcher curry doze buckles fuller slob darn tutor peg-pan an feeder pegs. Yap, fodder, are fetter pegs.

Ditcher mail-car caws an swoop otter caw staple. Off curse, Fodder. Are mulct oiler caws an swapped otter staple, an fetter checkings, an clammed upper larder oiler aches, an wen darn tutor vestibule guarding toe peck oiler bogs an warms offer vestibules, an watched an earned yore closing, an fetter hearses.

Ditcher warder oiler hearses, toe. enter-ruptured oiled Huskings. Nor, Fodder, are dint. Dint warder mar hearses? Wire nut.

Oil-wares tarred, crumpled Huskings. Wail, sense yore sore tarred, oil lecher wrestle ladle, bought *gad offer debt cheer.* Wile yore wrestling, yore kin maker bets an washer dashes.

Suture fodder. Effervescent fur Violate's sweathard, Hairy Parkings, disk pore gull word sordidly half ban furry musible.
MOANLATE AN ROACHES
Violate worse jest wile aboard Hairy, hoe worse jester pore form bore firming adjourning form. Sum pimple set debt Hairy Parkings dint half gut since, butter hatter gut dispossession an

hay worse medley an luff wet Violate. Infect, Hairy wandered toe merrier, butter worse toe skirt toe aster.

Wan gnat Hairy an Violate war setting honor Huskings' beck perch inner moanlate, holing hens.

O hairy, crate Violate, jest locket debt putty moan. Arsenate rheumatic. Yap, inserted Hairy, lurking adder moan.

O hairy, contingent Violate, jest snuff doze flagrant orders combing firmer putty rat roaches inner floor guarding. Conjure small doze orders, hairy? Conjure small debt deletitious flagrancy. Yap, set Hairy, snuffing, lacquer haunting dug haunting fur rapids.

Lessen hairy, whiskered Violate, arm oilmoist shore yore gut sum-sing toe asthma. Denture half sumsing impertinent toe asthma, hairy. Denture?

Pore hairy, skirt oilmoist artifice wets, stuttered toe trample, butter poled hamshelf toegadder, an gargled, "Ark, yap, Violate are gas are gas are gut sum-sing. O shocks, Violate.

Gore earn, hairy, gore earn, encysted Violate, gadding impassioned. Dun bay sore inhabited. Nor, den, watcher garner asthma.

Wail, Violate, arm jester pore form bore, an dun half mush moaning. Hoe cars aboard moaning. Pimple dun heifer bay retch toe gat merit, bought day order lack itch udder. Merit cobbles hoe lack itch udder gadder lung mush batter den udder cobbles hoe dun lack itch udder. Merit pimple order bay congenital, an arm shore, debt wail hay furry congenital an contended, an, fur debt raisin, way dun heifer half mush moaning."

Furry lung, lung, term disk harpy cobble set honor beck perch inner moanlate, holing hens an snuffing flagrant orders firmer floors inner floor guarding. Finely Violate set, bought lessen, hairy—inner moaning yore gutter asthma fodder.

Radar, conjure gas wart hopping? Hairy aster fodder, hoe exploded wet anchor an setter larder furry bat warts. Infect, haze languish worse jest hobble. Yonder nor sorghum-stenches wad disk stenchy.

Violate lift wetter fodder, oiled Former Huskings, hoe hatter repetition fur bang furry retch—an furry stenchy. Infect,

pimple orphan set debt Violate's fodder worse nosing button oiled mouser. Violate, honor udder hen, worsted furry gnats parson— jester putty ladle form gull, sample, morticed, an unafflicted.

Wan moaning Former Huskings nudist haze dodder setting honor cheer, during nosing. *Violate!* shorted dole former, watcher setting darn fur. Denture nor yore canned gat retch setting darn during nosing. Germ pup otter debt cheer.

Arm tarred, fodder, resplendent Violate warily.

Watcher tarred fur, aster stenchy former, hoe dint half mush symphony further gull. Are badger dint doe mush woke disk moaning. Ditcher curry doze buckles fuller slob darn tutor peg-pan an feeder pegs. Yap, fodder, are fetter pegs.

Ditcher mail-car caws an swoop otter caw staple. Off curse, Fodder. Are mulct oiler caws an swapped otter staple, an fetter checkings, an clammed upper larder inner checking-horse toe gadder oiler aches, an wen darn tutor vestibule guarding toe peck oiler bogs an warms offer vestibules, an watched an earned yore closing, an fetter hearses.

Ditcher warder oiler hearses, toe. enter-ruptured oiled Huskings. Nor, Fodder, are dint. Dint warder mar hearses? Wire nut.

Oil-wares tarred, crumpled Huskings. Wail, sense yore sore tarred, oil lecher wrestle ladle, bought *gad offer debt cheer.* Wile yore wrestling, yore kin maker bets an washer dashes.

Suture fodder. Effervescent fur Violate's sweathard, Hairy Parkings, disk pore gull word sordidly half ban furry musible.
MOANLATE AN ROACHES
Violate worse jest wile aboard Hairy, hoe worse jester pore form bore firming adjourning form. Sum pimple set debt Hairy Parkings dint half gut since, butter hatter gut dispossession an hay worse medley an luff wet Violate. Infect, Hairy wandered toe merrier, butter worse toe skirt toe aster.

Wan gnat Hairy an Violate war setting honor Huskings' beck perch inner moanlate, holing hens.

O hairy, crate Violate, jest locket debt putty moan. Arsenate rheumatic. Yap, inserted Hairy, lurking adder moan.

O hairy, contingent Violate, jest snuff doze flagrant orders combing firmer putty rat roaches inner floor guarding. Conjure small doze orders, hairy? Conjure small debt deletitious flagrancy. Yap, set Hairy, snuffing, lacquer haunting dug haunting fur rapids.

Lessen hairy, whiskered Violate, arm oilmoist shore yore gut sum-sing toe asthma. Denture half sumsing impertinent toe asthma, hairy. Denture?

Pore hairy, skirt oilmoist artifice wets, stuttered toe trample, an gargled, "Ark, yap, Violate are gas are gas are gut sum-sing. O shocks, Violate.

Gore earn, hairy, gore earn, encysted Violate, gadding impassioned. Dun bay sore inhabited. Nor, den, watcher garner asthma.

Wail, Violate, arm jester pore form bore, an dun half mush moaning. Hoe cars aboard moaning. Pimple dun heifer bay retch toe gat merit, bought day order lack itch udder. Merit violate worse jest wile aboard Hairy, hoe worse jester pore form bore firming adjourning form. Sum pimple set debt Hairy Parkings dint half gut since, butter hatter gut dispossession an hay worse medley an luff wet Violate. Infect, Hairy wandered toe merrier, butter worse toe skirt toe aster.

Wan gnat Hairy an Violate war setting honor Huskings' beck perch inner moanlate, holing hens.

O hairy, crate Violate, jest locket debt putty moan. Arsenate rheumatic. Yap, inserted Hairy, lurking adder moan.

O hairy, contingent Violate, jest snuff doze flagrant orders combing firmer putty rat roaches inner floor guarding. Conjure small doze orders, hairy? Conjure small debt deletitious flagrancy. Yap, set Hairy, snuffing, lacquer haunting dug haunting fur rapids.

Lessen hairy, whiskered Violate, arm oilmoist shore yore gut sum-sing toe asthma. Denture half sumsing impertinent toe asthma, hairy. Denture?

Pore hairy, skirt oilmoist artifice wets, stuttered toe trample, butter poled hamshelf toegadder, an gargled, "Ark, yap, Violate are gas are gas are gut sum-sing. O shocks, Violate. Ditcher warder oiler hearses, toe. enter-ruptured

This is a pretty intimidating block of text. As a reader, you would have to be seriously interested in the information to get through the entire piece; can you imagine if there were a dozen or so pages like this? For some projects, massive quantities of clean, unbroken text is perfectly acceptable, but be realistic about your readers.

Even if there are no graphics to break up the monotony of gray blocks of text, you can use type to add visual interest to the page. If readers are not interested in this particular article, their eyes will still be attracted to the bolder and bigger type and they will at least scan the information. Below is a list of other changes we made to this page:

VIOLATE HUSKINGS *by H. L. Chace*

Ore ornery aboard inner gelded ketch. Aye rheumatic starry.

Darn Honor Form

Heresy rheumatic starry off former's dodder, Violate Huskings, an wart hoppings darn honor form.

Violate lift wetter fodder, oiled Former Huskings, hoe hatter repetition fur bang furry retch—an furry stenchy. Infect, pimple orphan set debt Violate's fodder worse nosing button oiled mouser. Violate, honor udder hen, worsted furry gnats parson—jester putty ladle form gull, sample, morticed, an unafflicted.

Wan moaning Former Huskings nudist haze dodder setting honor cheer, during nosing. *Violatel* shorted dole former, watcher setting darn fur. Denture nor yore canned gat retch setting darn during nosing. Germ pup otter debt cheer.

Arm tarred, fodder, resplendent Violate warily.

Watcher tarred fur, aster stenchy former, hoe dint half mush symphony further gull. Are badger dint doe mush woke disk moaning. Ditcher curry doze buckles fuller slob darn tutor peg-pan an feeder pegs. Yap, fodder, are fetter pegs.

MAILCAR CAWS AND SWOOP OTTER CAW STAPLE.

Ditcher mailcar caws an swoop otter caw staple. Off curse, Fodder. Are mulct oiler caws an swapped otter staple, an fetter checkings, an clammed upper larder inner checking-horse toe gadder oiler aches, an wen darn tutor vestibule guarding.

Ditcher warder oiler hearses, toe, enter-ruptured oiled Huskings. Nor, Fodder, are dint. Dint warder mar hearses? Wire nut.

Oil-wares tarred, crumpled Huskings. Wail, sense yore sore tarred, oil lecher wrestle ladle, bought *god offer debt cheer.* Wile yore wrestling, yore kin maker bets an washer dashes.

Suture fodder. Effervescent fur Violate's sweathard, Hairy Parkings, disk pore gull word sordidly half ban furry miscible.

Moanlate an Roaches

Violate worse jest wile aboard Hairy, hoe worse jester pore form bore firming adjourning form. Sum pimple set debt Hairy Parkings dint half gut since, butter hatter gut dispossession an hay worse medley an luff wet Violate. Infect, Hairy wandered toe merrier, butter worse toe skirt toe aster.

Wan gnat Hairy an Violate war setting honor Huskings' beck perch inner moanlate, holing dare hens.

O hairy, crate Violate, jest locket debt putty moan. Arsenate rheumatic. Yap, inserted Hairy, lurking adder moan.

O hairy, contingent Violate, jest snuff doze flagrant orders, combing firmer putty rat roaches inner floor guarding. Conjure small doze orders, hairy? Conjure small debt deletitious flagrancy. Snuffing, lacquer haunting dug haunting fur peck hairy rapids.

Lessen hairy, whiskered Violate, arm oilmoist shore yore gut sum-sing toe asthma. Denture half sumsing impertinent toe asthma, hairy. Denture? Pore hairy, skirt oilmoist artifice wets, stuttered toe trample, butter poled hamshelf toegadder, an gargled, "Ark, yap, Violate are gas are gas are gut sum-sing. O shocks violate.

Gore earn, hairy, gore earn, encysted Violate, gadding impassioned. Dun bay sore inhabited. Nor, den, watcher garner asthma.

Wail, Violate, arm jester pore form bore, an dun half mush moaning. Hoe cars aboard moaning. Pimple dun heifer bay retch toe gat merit, bought day order lack itch udder. Merit cobbles hoe lack itch udder gadder lung mush batter den udder cobbles hoe dun lack itch udder. Merit pimple order bay congenital, an arm shore, debt wail bay furry congenital an contended, an, fur debt raisin, way dun heifer half mush moaning."

Conjure Gas

Furry lung, lung, term disk harpy cobble set honor beck perch inner moanlate, holing hens an snuffing flagrant orders firmer floors inner floor guarding. Firmly Violate sets, bought lessen, hairy—inner moaning yore gutter asthma hole fodder.

Radar, conjure gas wart hopping? Hairy aster fodder, hoe exploited wet anchor an setter larder furry bat warts. Infect, haze languish worse jest hobble. Yonder nor sorghum-stenches wad disk stenchy. Violate lift wetter fodder, oiled Former Huskings, hoe hatter repetition fur bang furry retch—

an furry stenchy. Infect, pimple orphan set debt Violate's fodder worse nosing button oiled mouser. Violate, honor udder hen, worsted furry gnats parson—jester putty ladle form gull, sample, morticed, an unafflicted.

Wan moaning Former Huskings nudist haze dodder setting honor cheer, during nosing. *Violatel* shorted dole former, watcher setting darn fur. Denture nor yore canned gat retch setting darn during nosing. Germ pup otter debt cheer.

Arm tarred, fodder, resplendent Violate warily.

Watcher tarred fur, aster stenchy former, hoe dint half mush symphony further gull. Are badger dint doe mush woke disk moaning. Ditcher curry

JEST SNUFF DOZE FLAGRANT ORDERS.

doze buckles fuller slob darn tutor peg-pan an feeder pegs. Yap, fodder, are fetter pegs.

Ditcher mail-car caws an swoop otter caw staple. Off curse, Fodder. Are mulct oiler caws swapped otter staple, an fetter checkings, an clammed upper larder inner checking-horse toe gadder oiler aches, an wen darn tutor vestibule guarding toe peck oiler bogs an washer earned yore closing, an fetter hearses.

—continued own patch 5

Obviously, this sort of type manipulation is appropriate for items like newsletters, newspapers, magazines, and brochures, while it is not appropriate for items like novels. In a novel, the reader *wants* to read huge amounts of uninterrupted text.

▸ There are some resting spots of white space that help to open up the page.

▸ The flush left alignment, instead of justified, not only makes the text easier to read, but it also allows more white space to filter into the piece.

▸ Adding a little more linespace lightens the look of the page and makes it less forbidding.

▸ Using space between paragraphs instead of an indent also helps to open it up and make each individual paragraph more tempting to read because the reader doesn't feel like he is making such a commitment: "Okay, I'll just read this one paragraph." Which leads to the next, of course.

Several of these manipulations mean you will have less text on the page. If this is a problem for your project, know that it is possible to open up the text, lighten the page, and create a more appealing look and still get as many words on the page. Try a condensed typeface, a face with a smaller x-height, or don't add quite so much linespace (for instance, try 12.4 instead of 12.7 points of leading). It is always possible to make readable type.

Don'ts

Below is a list of things *not* to do when setting a quantity of text.

❶ If you indent the paragraphs, *do not* indent the first paragraph following a headline or subhead. The indent is a clue that there's a new paragraph starting, but after a head or subhead, that clue is redundant.

❷ Either add "paragraph space after" (as described below) *or* use an indent—not both!

❸ Don't use a double-Return between paragraphs. It creates too much space between the related items. In fact, there is almost never an excuse to hit that Return/Enter key twice—learn to use your software. Every program has a feature in which you can add extra space after paragraphs. For instance, if your text is set 10.5/13, add about half of the linespace (which would be about 6 points) between paragraphs: in your style sheet definition, set the amount of space to *follow* a paragraph (it might be called something like "paragraph space after") as 6 points.

VIOLATE HUSKINGS

Ore ornery aboard inner gelded ketch. Aye rheumatic starry.

DARN HONOR FORM

❶ Heresy rheumatic starry offer former's dodder, Violate Huskings, an wart hoppings darn honor form.

❷ Violate lift wetter fodder, oiled Former Huskings, hoe hatter repetition fur bang furry retch—an furry stenchy. Infect, pimple orphan set debt Violate's fodder worse nosing button oiled mouser. Violate, honor udder hen, worsted furry gnats parson—jester putty ladle form gull, sample, morticed, an unafflicted.

❸ Wan moaning Former Huskings nudist Jack dodder setting honor cheer, during nosing. *Violatel* shorted dole former, watcher setting darn fur. Denture nor yore canned gat retch setting darn during nosing. Germ pup otter debt cheer.

Arm tarred, fodder, resplendent Violate warily.

Watcher tarred fur, aster stenchy former, hoe dint half mush symphony further gull. Are badger

❹ dint doe mush woke disk moaning. Ditcher curry doze buckles fuller slob darn tutor peg-pan an feeder pegs. Yap, fodder, are fetter pegs.

Ditcher mail-car caws an swoop otter caw staple. Off curse, Fodder. Are mulct oiler caws an swapped otter staple, an fetter checkings, an clammed upper larder inner checking-horse toe gadder oiler aches, an wen darn tutor vestibule guarding toe peck oiler bogs an warms offer vestibules, an watched an earned yore closing, an fetter hearses.

Ditcher warder oiler hearses, toe. enter-ruptured oiled Huskings. Nor, Fodder, are dint. Dint warder mar hearses? Wire nut. ❺

OIL-WARES TARRED

Oil-wares tarred, crumpled Huskings. Wail, sense yore sore tarred, oil lecher wrestle ladle, bought *gad offer debt cheer.* Wile yore wrestling, yore kin maker bets an washer dashes.

Suture fodder. Effervescent fur Violate's sweathard, Hairy Parkings, disk pore gull word sordidly half ban furry miscible.

MOANLATE AN ROACHES

Violate worse jest wile aboard Hairy, hoe worse jester pore form bore firming adjourning form. Sum pimple set debt Hairy Parkings dint half gut since, butter hatter gut dispossession an hay worse medley an luff wet Violate. Infect, Hairy wandered toe merrier, butter worse toe skirt toe aster.

Wan gnat Hairy an Violate war setting honor Huskings' beck perch inner moanlate, holing hens.

O hairy, crate Violate, jest locket debt putty moan. Arsenate rheumatic. Yap, inserted Hairy, lurking adder moan.

O hairy, contingent Violate, jest snuff doze flagrant orders combing firmer putty rat roaches inner floor guarding. Conjure small doze orders, hairy? Conjure small debt deletitious flagrancy. Yap, set Hairy, snuffing, lacquer haunting dug haunting fur rapids.

Lessen hairy, whiskered Violate, arm oil moist shore yore gut sum-sing toe asthma. Denture half sumsing impertinent toe asthma, hairy. Denture?

Pore hairy, skirt oilmoist artifice wets, stuttered toe trample, butter poled hamshelf toegadder, an gargled, "Are gas are gas are gut sum-sing.

Gore earn, hairy, gore earn, encysted Violate, gadding impassioned. Dun bay sore inhabited. Nor, den, watcher garner asthma.

HOE CARS ABOARD MOANING

Wail, Violate, arm jester pore form bore, an dun half mush moaning. Hoe cars aboard moaning. Pimple dun heifer bay retch toe gat merit, bought day order lack itch udder. Merit cobbles hoe lack itch udder gadder lung mush batter den udder cobbles hoe dun lack itch udder. Merit pimple order bay congenital, an arm shore, debt wail bay furry congenital an contended, an, fur debt raisin, way dun heifer half mush moaning."

Furry lung, lung, term disk harpy cobble set honor beck perch inner moanlate, holing hens an snuffing flagrant orders firmer floors inner floor guarding. Finely Violate set, bought ❼ lessen, hairy—inner moaning yore gutter asthma fodder.

Radar, conjure gas wart hopping? Hairy aster fodder, hoe exploited wet anchor an setter larder furry bat warts. Infect, haze

PAGE 3 • MAY NEWSLETTER ❻

---

❹ Either bottom out the columns (align the last lines all on the same baseline) or don't—but do not *almost* align them. Almost doesn't count. You do not have to fill every column to the bottom, but if you don't, then make the nice, open, white space look like a conscious design element, not a mistake.

❺ Follow the basic guidelines for good typography and leave no widows, orphans, or awkward line breaks.

❻ Don't emphasize elements that are not that important. For instance, the page numbers can be small, and they certainly don't need the word "page" set next to them—readers understand it's a page. Now, we're not saying page numbers are not important—of course they are. But they don't need to be set in 12-point type. Readers will find the page numbers easily if they are 8 or 9 point and consistently placed in the same place on every page. By de-emphasizing their importance visually, you can give more importance to the text on the page.

❼ Don't justify text on a short line; it creates terrible and inconsistent word and letter spacing. If you really want or need a justified look, be sure to use a column wide enough to avoid those awful gaps between words or scrunched letter spacing.

Dos

Below is a list of things to do when setting a quantity of text.

❶ Use contrast to emphasize headlines so a reader can scan them easily. If you need more visual interest without graphics, use contrast to call out important words in an article and pull a reader's eyes into the piece.

❷ If you don't have many headlines, avoid a text-heavy look by using pull quotes.

❸ Use more space *above* heads and subheads and less space *below*. This follows the rule of proximity: the headline or subhead should be closer to the paragraph it belongs with and farther away from the paragraph above it.

❹ Align every item on the page with some other element on the page (for instance, align the rules with the column edges). If you choose to break the alignment principle, then break it with gusto—if you're a wimp (say you misalign an element by ¼ inch), it will look like a mistake.

Violate Huskings

Ore ornery aboard inner gelded ketch. Aye rheumatic starry.

❶ **Darn Honor Form**

Heresy rheumatic starry offer former's dodder, Violate Huskings, an wart hoppings darn honor form.

Violate lift wetter fodder, oiled Former Huskings, hoe hatter repetition fur bang furry retch—an furry stenchy. Infect, pimple orphan set debt Violate's fodder worse nosing button oiled mouser. Violate, honor udder hen, worsted gnats parson—jester puny ladle form gull, sample, morticed, an unafflicted.

Wan moaning Former Huskings nudist haze dodder setting honor cheer, during nosing. Violatel shorted dole former, watcher setting darn fur. Denture nor yore canned gat retch setting darn during nosing. Germ pup otter debt cheer.

Arm tarred, fodder, resplend Violate warily.

Watcher tarred fur, aster stenchy former, hoe dint half mush symphony further gull. Are badger dint doe mush woke disk moaning. Ditcher curry doze buckles fuller slob darn tutor peg-pan en feeder pegs. Yap, fodder, are fetter pegs.

Ditcher mail-car caws an swoop otter caw staple. Offcurse, Fodder. Are mulct oiler caws an swapped otter staple, an fetter checkings, an clammed upper larder inner checking-horse toe gadder oiler aches, an wen darn tutor vestibule guarding toe peck oiler bogs an warms offer vestibules, an watched an earned yore closing, an fetter hearses. Pore hairy, skirt oilmoist artifice wets, stuttered toe trample.

Ditcher warder oiler hearses, toe. enter-ruptured oiled Huskings. Nor, Fodder, are dint. Dint warder mar hearses? Wire nut. ❸

Oil-wares Tarred

Oil-wares tarred, crumpled Huskings. Wail, sense yore sore tarred, oil lecher wrestle ladle, bought gad offer debt cheer. Wile yore wrestling, yore kin maker bets an washer dashes.

Suture fodder. Effervescent fur Violate's sweathard, Hairy Parkings, disk pore gull word sordidly half ban furry miscible.

Moanlate an Roaches

Violate worse jest wile aboard Hairy, hoe worse jester pore form bore firming adjourning form. Sum pimple set debt Hairy Parkings dint half gut since, butter hatter gut dispossession an hay worse medley an luff wet Violate. Infect, Hairy wandered toe merrier, butter worse toe skirt toe aster.

Wan gnat Hairy an Violate war setting honor Huskings' beck perch inner moanlate, holing dare hens. Oh hairy, crate Violate, jest locket debt putty moan. Arsenate rheumatic.

Center Alley ❺

Center alley worse jester pore ladle gull hoe lift wetter stop-murder an toe heft-cisterns. Daze worming war furry wicket an shellfish parsons, spatially dole stop-murder, hoe dint lack Center Alley an, infect, word orphan traitor pore gull mar lichen ammonol dinner rail hormone bang.

Oily inner moaning disk wicket oiled worming shorted, "Center Alley, gad otter bet an goiter wark! Suture bat lacy ladle bomb! Shaker lake!" An firm moaning tell gnat disk ratchet gull word heifer wark lacquer hearse toe kipper horsing ardor, washer heft-cistern's closing, maker bets, gore tutor star fur perversions, cooker males, washer dashes, an doe oily udder hoard wark. Nor wander pore Center Alley worse tarred an disgorged!

Nor wander pore Center Alley ❷ worse tarred!

Wan moaning, Center Alley herder heft-cisterns tucking a boarder bag boil debtor prance worse garner gift toiler pimple inner lend.

"O stop-murder," crater ladle gull, "Water swill cerebration debt boil's garner bayl! Are sordidly ward lacquer goiter debt boil!"

"Shed dope, Center Alley," inserter curl stop-murder. Yore tucking lichen end-bustle! Yore nutty goring tore debt boil—armor goring tutor boi. ❻

❹

Be consistent with the layout and design elements. Then if you want to break out of that consistency, be brave and bold with the inconsistency so it is obviously a design feature and not a bug.

❺ Find elements that repeat (rules, headlines styles, captions, bullets) and emphasize their design features; the repetition will unify the various pages.

❻ Use a grid with several columns so you can have flexibility in your layout. The page above is actually divided into six columns. As you can see, the different stories use different combinations of those six columns. There are more examples of using a simple grid on the next few pages.

Within the image:

Ladle Rat Rotten Hut

Wants pawn term dare worsted ladle gull hoe lift wetter murder inner ladle cordage honor itch offer lodge, dock, florist. Disk ladle gull orphan worry Putty ladle rat cluck wetter ladle rat hut, an fur disk raisin pimple colder Ladle Rat Rotten Hut.

Wan moaning Ladle Rat Rotten Hut's murder colder inset. "Ladle Rat Rotten Hut, heresy ladle basking winsome burden barter an shirker cockles. Tick disk ladle basking tutor cordage offer groin-murder hoe lifts honor udder site offer florist. Shaker lake! Dun stopper laundry wrote! Dun stopper peck floors! Dun daily-doily inner florist, an yonder nor sorghum-stenches, dun stopper torque wet strainers!"

"Hoe-cake, murder," resplendent Ladle Rat Rotten Hut, an tickle ladle basking an stuttered oft.

Honor wrote tutor cordage offer groin-murder, Ladle Rat Rotten Hut mitten anomalous woof.

"Wail, wail, waill" set disk wicket woof, "Evanescent Ladle Rat Rotten Hut! Wares are putty ladle gull goring wizard ladle basking?"

"Armor goring tumor groin-murder's," reprisal ladle gull. "Grammar's seeking bet. Armor ticking arson burden barter an shirker cockles."

"0 bore! Heifer gnats woke," setter wicket woof, butter taught tomb shelf, "Oil tickle shirt court tutor cordage offer groin-murder. Oil ketchup wetter letter, an den—O bore!" Soda wicket woof tucker shirt court, an whinny retched a cordage offer groin-murder, picked

inner windrow, an sore debtor pore oil worming worse lion inner bet. Inner flesh, disk abdominal woof lipped honor bet, paunched honor pore oil worming, an garbled erupt. Den disk ratchet ammonol pot honor groin-murder's nut cup an gnat-gun, any curdled ope inner bet.

Inner ladle wile, Ladle Rat Rotten Hut a raft attar cordage an ranker dough ball. "Comb ink, sweat hard," setter wicket woof, disgracing is verse.

Ladle Rat Rotten Hut entity bet rum an stud buyer groin-murder's bet.

"O Grammarl" crater ladle gull historically, "Water bag icer gut! A nervous sausage bag ice!"

"Battered lucky chew whiff, sweat hard," setter bloat-Thursday woof, wetter wicket small honors phase.

O, Grammar, water bag noise! A nervous sore suture anomalous prognosis!"

"Battered small your whiff, doling,"

Hormone Derange

O gummier hum
  warder buffer-lore rum
Enter dare enter envelopes ply,
Ware soiled'em assured
  adage cur-itching ward
An disguise earn a clotty oil die.
Harm, hormone derange,
Warder dare enter envelopes ply,
Ware soiled'em assured
  adage cur-itching ward
An disguise earn a clotty oil die.

Guilty Looks Enter Tree Beers

Wants pawn term dare worsted ladle gull hoe hat search putty yowler coils debt pimple colder Guilty Looks.

Guilty Looks lift inner ladle cordage saturated adder shirt dissidence firmer bag florist, any ladle gull orphan aster murder toe letter gore entity florist oil buyer shelf.

"Guilty Looks!" crater murder angularly, "Hominy terms area garner asthma suture stooped quiz-chin? Goiter door florist?

Sordidly nut!"

"Wire nut, murder?" wined Guilty Looks, hoe dint peony tension tore murder's scaldings.

"Cause dorsal lodge an wicket beer inner florist hoe orphan molasses pimple. Ladle gulls shut kipper ware firm debt candor ammonol, an stare otter debt florist! Debt florist's mush toe dentures furry ladle gull!"

Wail, pimple oil-wares wander doe wart udder pimple dum wampum toe doe. Debt's jest hormone nurture. Wan moaning, Guilty Looks dissipater murder, an win entity

Dun stopper torque wet strainers!

Center Alley Worse Jester Pore Ladle Gull

Center alley worse jester pore ladle gull hoe lift wetter stop-murder an toe heft-cisterns. Daze worming war furry wicket an shellfish parsons, spatially dole stop-murder, hoe dint lack Center Alley an, infect, word orphan traitor pore gull mar lichen ammonol dinner hormone bang.

Oily inner moaning disk wicket oiled worming shorted, "Center Alley, gad otter bet an goiter wark! Suture lacy ladle bomb! Shaker lake!" An firm moaning tell gnat disk ratchet gull word heifer wark lacquer hearse toe kipper horsing ardor, washer heft-cistern's closing, maker bets, gore tutor star fur perversions, cooker males, washer dashes, an doe oily udder board wark. Nor wander pore Center Alley worse tarred an disgorged!

Soddenly, Center Alley nudist debt annulled worming hat entity rum an worse setting buyer site. Disk oiled worming worry furry gourd-murder. "Center Alley, Center Alley," whiskered dole worming, "watcher crane aboard? Ditcher wander goiter debt boil? Hoe-cake, jest goiter yore gardening an pickle bag pomp-can; den goiter yore staple an gutter bag rattletrap witch contends sex anomalous ratch. Wail, watcher wading fur? Gat goring!"

Center Alley garter pomp-can any sex bag ratch. Inner flesh, dole worming chintz door pomp-can intern anomalous, gorges, courage. Dingy chintz door sex beg ratch enter sex wide hearses. Oil offer sodden, Center Alley real-iced dashy worse warring putty an

Wan moaning, Center Alley herder heft-cisterns tucking a boarder bag boil debtor prance worse garner gift toiler pimple inner lend.

"O stop-murder," crater ladle gull, "Water swill cerebration debt boil's garner bay! Are sordidly ward lacquer goiter debt boil!"

"Shed dope, Center Alley," inserter curl stop-murder, "Yore tucking lichen end-bustle! Yore nutty goring tore debt boil—armor goring tutor boil wet yore toe heft-cisterns. Yore garner stair rat hair an kipper horsing ardor an washer pods an pens! Gore tutor boil? Hoar, hoar! Locket yore close—nosing bought racks!"

Soda wicket stop-murder any toe ogling cisterns pot honor expansive closing, an stuttered oft tutor boil, living pore Center Alley setting buyer far inner racket closing, wit tares strumming darner chicks.

Door wicket stop-murder wore trampling wet forestation.

expansive closing—sulk an sadden—an honor ladle fate war toe putty ladle gloss slobbers.

Center Alley, harpy acid lurk, clammed entity gorges courage, any sex wide hearses gobbled aware tutor prance's boil.

"0 borel" crater prance, whinny sore Center Alley, "Hoes disk putty ladle checking wetter gloss slobbers?" Any win ope toe Center Alley an aster furry dense, den fur servile udders. Door prance dint wander dense wet dodder gulls—jest wet Center Alley.

Pimple whiskered, "Jest locket debt gnats-lurking cobbler. Door prance sordidly enter-stance harder peck gut-lurking worming!"

Ladle Center Alley worse door bail offer boil.

Door wicket stop-murder any toe ogling cisterns wore trampling wet anchor an forestation.

"Courses, courses!" crater stop-murder. "Hoes debt ladle Manx wetter

Center Alley, harpy acid lurk.

There are several common problems with this very typical spread:

› It's locked into the three-column spread. See the following examples for multiple-column formats and how they expand your design possibilities.

› There is superfluous stuff at the top of the pages. If this is a 4-page newsletter, it is completely unnecessary to label pages 2 and 3—readers know it is page 2 or 3. If this is a large newsletter, you need the page number but you don't need the word "page."
Readers know it is a page and they know that little number in the corner is the page number.

Readers also know which publication they are holding at the moment so you can eliminate the reminder at the top. The more junk you can eliminate, the more design options you will have.

› The page is crowded at the top with junk and the text is crowded too close to the bottom rule.

› The photographs are nice, but they are "sort of" tucked into the columns. Either tuck them in completely, smoothly aligned with the column edges, or break them out of the column edges with gusto. "Almost" looks like a mistake.

› Each of the photos has the same visual impact. Make something dominant.

› The bottoms of the columns "almost" align. Don't do "almost." Either *do it* and align them right on the same line, or *don't do it* and make it very clear they are not aligned.

On the positive side, the headlines have good contrast with the type; the text is readable and flush left instead of being forced into a justified alignment.

Ladle Rat Rotten Hut

Wants pawn term dare worsted ladle gull hoe lift wetter murder inner ladle cordage honor itch offer lodge, dock, florist. Disk ladle gull orphan worry Putty ladle rat cluck wetter ladle rat hut, an fur disk raisin pimple colder Ladle Rat Rotten Hut.

Wan moaning Ladle Rat Rotten Hut's murder colder inset. "Ladle Rat Rotten Hut, heresy ladle basking winsome burden barter an shirker cockles. Tick disk ladle basking tutor cordage offer groin-murder hoe lifts honor udder site offer florist. Shaker lake! Dun stopper laundry wrote! Dun daily-doily inner florist, an yonder nor sorghum-stenches, dun stopper torque wet strainers!"

"Hoe-cake, murder," resplendent Ladle Rat Rotten Hut, an tickle ladle basking an stuttered oft. Honor wrote tutor cordage offer groin-murder, Ladle Rat Rotten Hut mitten anomalous woof.

"Wail, wail, waill" set disk wicket woof, "Evanes-cent Ladle Rat Rotten Hut! Wares are putty ladle gull goring wizard ladle basking?"

"Armor goring tumor groin-murder's," reprisal ladle gull. "Grammar's seeking bet. Armor tick-ing arson burden barter an shirker cockles."

"O hoe! Heifer gnats woke," setter wicket woof, butter taught tomb shelf, "Oil tickle shirt court tutor cordage offer groin-murder. Oil ketchup wetter letter, an den—O bore!"

Soda wicket woof tucker shirt court, an whinny retched a cordage offer groin-murder, picked inner windrow, an sore debtor pore oil worming worse lion inner bet. Inner flesh, disk abdominal woof lipped honor bet, paunched honor pore oil worming, an garbled erupt. Den disk ratchet ammonol pot honor groin-murder's nut cup an gnat-gun, any curdled ope inner bet.

Tick disk ladle basking tutor cordage offer groin-murder.

Guilty Looks Enter Tree Beers

Wants pawn term dare wor-sted ladle gull hoe hat search putty yowler coils debt pimple colder Guilty Looks.

Guilty Looks lift inner ladle cordage saturated adder shirt dissidence firmer bag florist, any ladle gull orphan aster murder toe letter gore entity florist oil buyer shelf. "Guilty Looks!" crater murder angu-larly, "Hominy terms area

—continued on page 8

Hormone Derange

O gummier hum
   warder buffer-lore rum
Enter dare enter envelopes ply,
Ware soiled 'em assured
   adage cur-itching ward
An disguise earn it clotty oil die.
Harm, hormone derange,
Warder dare enter envelopes ply,
Ware soiled 'em assured
   adage cur-itching ward
An disguise earn it clotty oil die.

Center Alley Worse Jester Pore Ladle Gull

Center alley worse jester pore ladle gull hoe lift wetter stop-murder an toe heft-cisterns. Daze worming war furry wicket an shellfish parsons, spatially dole stop-murder, hoe dint lack Center Alley an, infect, word orphan traitor pore gull mar lichen ammonol dinner hormone bang.

Oily inner moaning disk wicket oiled worming shorted, "Center Alley, gad otter bet an goiter wark! Suture lacy ladle bomb! Shaker lake!" An firm moaning tell gnat disk ratchet gull word heifer wark lacquer hearse toe kipper horsing ardor, washer heft-cistern's closing, maker bets, gore tutor star fur perversions, cooker males, washer dashes, an doe oily udder hoard wark. Nor wander pore Center Alley worse tarred an disgorged!

Center Alley setting buyer far inner racket closing.

Wan moaning, Center Alley herder heft-cisterns tucking a boarder bag boil debtor prance worse garner gift toiler pimple inner lead.

"O stop-murder," crater ladle gull, "Water swill celebration debt boil's garner bay! Are sordidly ward lacquer goiter debt boil!" Shed dope, center alley, inserter curl stop-murder. Yore tucking lichen end bustle.

Yore nutty goring tore debt boil—armor goring tutor boil wet yore toe heft-cisterns. Yore garner stair at hair an kipper horsing ardor an washer pods an pens. Gore tutor boil? Hoar, hoar! Locket yore close—nosing bought oiled racks.

Soda wicket stop-murder any toe ogling cisterns pot honor expansive closing, an stuttered oft tutor boil, living pore

Center Alley setting buyer far inner racket closing, wit tares strumming darner chicks.

Soddenly, Center Alley nudist debt annulled worming hat entity runs an worse setting buyer site. Disk oiled worming worry furry gourd-murder. Center Alley, whiskered dole worming, watcher crane aboard. Ditcher wander goiter debt boil? Hoe-cake, jest goiter

Farther wail fur arm moist.

Dare Ashy Turban Inner Torn

Dare ashy turban inner torn, inner torn, an dare mar dare luff set shim darn, set shim darn an drakes haze whine wet feller fray an nabber, nabber thanks off may. Farther wail fur arm moist leaf year. doughnut letter parroting grave year.

Enter member debtor bust off fronts moist port, moist port. Adjure, adjure, canned fronts, adjure, jess, adjure Are kin nor

lunger stare wet your, stare wet your. Oil hank mar hop honor warping wallow tray, an murder whirl gore wail wet they, wet they.

Farther wail fur arm moist leaf year. doughnut letter parroting grave year. Enter member debtor bust off fronts moist port, moist port. Adjure, adjure, canned fronts, adjure, jess, adjure Are kin nor lunger stare wet your.

This spread is looking a little better:

> Instead of a 3-column grid, we used a 7-column grid, as shown in the screen shot to the right. This gives us more flexibility in arranging the columns of text.

> We got rid of superfluous stuff.

> We opened up the space, gave more breathing room around all edges, added a wee bit of linespacing.

> We made one of the photos more dominant than the others.

> We aligned everything. Yes, it's like putting a puzzle together.

Ladle Rat Rotten Hut

Wants pawn term dare worsted ladle gull hoe lift wetter murder inner ladle cordage honor itch offer lodge, dock, florist. Disk ladle gull orphan worry putty ladle rat hut, an fur disk raisin pimple colder Ladle Rat Rotten Hut.

Wan moaning Ladle Rat Rotten Hut's murder colder inset. "Ladle Rat Rotten Hut, heresy ladle basking winsome burden barter an shirker cockles. Tick disk ladle basking tutor cordage offer groin-murder hoe lifts honor udder site offer florist. Shaker lake! Dun stopper laundry wrote! Dun daily-doily inner florist, an yonder nor sorghum-stenches, dun stopper torque wet strainers!"

"Hoe-cake, murder," resplendent Ladle Rat Rotten Hut, an tickle ladle

Tick disk ladle basking tutor cordage offer groin-murder.

Guilty Looks Enter Tree Beers

Wants pawn term dare worsted ladle gull hoe hat search putty yowler coils debt pimple colder Guilty Looks.

Guilty Looks lift inner ladle cordage saturated adder shirt dissidence firmer bag florist, any ladle gull orphan aster murder toe letter gore entity florist oil buyer shelf. "Guilty Looks!" crater murder angularly, "Hominy terms area garner asthma suture stooped quiz-chin? Goiter door florist? Sordidly nut!"

"Wire nut, murder?" wined Guilty Looks, hoe dint peony tension tore murder's scaldings.

"Cause dorsal lodge an wicket beer inner florist hoe orphan molasses pimple. Ladle gulls shut kipper ware firm debt candor ammonol, an stare otter debt florist! Debt florist's mush toe dentures furry ladle gull!" Wail, pimple oil-wares wander doe wart udder pimple dum

basking an stuttered oft. Honor wrote tutor cordage Ladle Rat Rotten Hut mitt anomalous woof.

Disk Wicket Woof

Wail, wail, waill, set disk wicket woof. Evanescent Ladle Rat Rotten Hut! Wares are putty ladle gull goring wizard ladle basking? Grammar's seeking bet. Armor ticking arson shirker cockles. O hoe! Heifer gnats woke, setter wicket woof.

wampum toe doe. Debt's jest hormone nurture. Wan moaning, Guilty Looks dissipater murder, an win entity florist.

Fur lung, disk avengeress gull wetter putty yowler coils cam tore morticed ladle cordage inhibited buyer bull firmly off beers—Fodder Beer (home pimple, fur oblivious raisins, coiled "Brewing"), Murder Beer, an Ladle Bore Beer. Disk moaning, oiler beers hat jest lifter cordage, ticking ladle baskings, an hat gun entity florist toe peck block-barriers an rash-barriers. Guilty Looks ranker dough ball; bought, off curse, nor-bawdy worse

—continued on page 8

HORMONE DERANGE

*O gummier hum
warder buffer-lore rum
Enter dare enter envelopes ply,
Ware soiled 'em assured
adage cur-itching ward
An disguise earn it clotty oil die.*

*Harm, hormone derange,
warder dare enter
envelopes ply,
Ware soiled 'em assured
adage cur-itching ward
An disguise earn it clotty oil die.*

Center Alley Worse Jester Pore Ladle Gull

Center alley worse jester pore ladle gull hoe lift wetter stop-murder an toe heft-cisterns. Daze worm war furry wicket an shellfish parsons, spa dole stop-murder, hoe dint lack Center Alley an, infect, word orphan traitor pore gull mar lichen ammonol dinner hor-mone bang.

Oily inner moaning disk wicket oiled worming shorted, "Center Alley, gad otter bet an goiter wark! Suture lacy ladle bomb! Shaker lake!" An firm moaning tell

gnat disk ratchet gull word heifer wark lacquer hearse toe kipper hors-ing ardor, washer heft-cistern's closing, maker bets, gore tutor star fur perver-sions, cooker males, washer dashes, an doe oily udder board wark. Nor wander pore Center Alley worse tarred an disgorged!

Wan moan-ing, Center Alley herder heft-cisterns tucking a boarder bag boil debtor prance worse

garner gift toiler pimple inner lend. "O stop murder," crater ladle gull, "Water swill cere-bration debt boil's garner bay! Are sordidly ward lacquer goiter debt boil!" Shed dope, center alley, inserter curl stopper-murder. Yore tucking

lichen end bustle. Yore nutty goring tore debt boil—armor goring tutor boil wet yore toe heft-cisterns. Yore garner stair rat hair an kipper hors-ing ardor an washer pods an pens. Gore tutor boil? Hoar, hoar! Locket yore close—nosing

bought oiled racks.

Soda wicket stop-murder any toe ogling cisterns pot honor expan-sive closing, an stuttered oft tutor boil, living pore Center Alley setting buyer far inner racket closing, wit tares strumming darner chicks. Soddenly not.

Dare Ashy Turban Inner Torn

Dare ashy turban inner torn, inner torn, an dare mar dare luff set shim darn, set shim darn an drakes haze whine wet lefter fray an nabher, nabher thanks off may. Farther wail fur arm moist leaf year. Doughnut letter parroting grave year.

Enter member debtor bust off fronts moist port, moist port. Adjure, adjure, canned fronts, adjure, jess, adjure. Are kin nor lunger stare wet your, stare wet your.

Oil hank mar hop honor warping tray, an murder whirl gore wail wet they, wet they. Are kin nor lunger stare wet your, stare wet your.

Farther wail fur arm moist leaf year. Doughnut letter parroting grave year. Enter member debtor bust off fronts moist port, moist port. Adjure, adjure, canned fronts, adjure, jess, adjure. Are kin nor lunger stare wet your.

Farther wail fur arm moist.

As we've mentioned several times on the previous pages, one simple design and layout technique that gives you a lot of flexibility in layout is to use a grid. If you have worked with grid theory before, you know it can be a complex solution for complex projects, and it works wonders. But you can also use a very simple grid, such as a multiple-column layout, and implement it in a simple manner.

This example uses the same 7-column layout as on the previous page. The layout options are endless.

Hormone Derange

O gummier hum
  warder buffer-lore rum
Enter dare enter envelopes ply,
Ware soiled 'em assured
  adage cur-itching ward
An disguise earn it clotty oil die.

Harm, hormone derange,
  warder dare enter
  envelopes ply,
Ware soiled 'em assured
  adage cur-itching ward
An disguise earn it clotty oil die.

Ladle Rat Rotten Hut

Wants pawn term dare worsted ladle gull hoe lift wetter murder inner ladle cordage honor itch offer lodge, dock, florist. Disk ladle gull orphan worry putty ladle rat hut, an fur disk raisin pimple colder Ladle Rat Rotten Hut.

Wan moaning Ladle Rat Rotten Hut's murder colder inset. "Ladle Rat Rotten Hut, heresy ladle basking winsome burden barter an shirker cockles. Tick disk ladle basking tutor cordage offer groin-murder hoe lifts honor udder site offer florist. Shaker lake! Dun stopper laundry wrote! Dun stopper peck floors! Dun daily-doily inner florist, an yonder nor sorghum-stenches, dun stopper torque wet strainers!"

"Hoe-cake, murder," resplendent Ladle Rat Rotten Hut, an tickle ladle basking an stuttered oft. Honor wrote tutor cordage Ladle Rat Rotten Hut mitt anomalous woof.

Disk Wicket Woof

Wail, wail, wail, set disk wicket woof. Evanescent Ladle Rat Rotten Hut! Wares are putty ladle gull goring wizard ladle basking! Grammar's seeking bet.Armor ticking arson shirker cockles. 0 hoe! Heifer gnats woke, setter wicket woof. Butter taught tomb shelf, oil tickle shirt court.

Guilty Looks Enter Tree Beers

Wants pawn term dare worsted ladle gull hoe hat search putty yowler coils debt pimple colder Guilty Looks. Guilty Looks lift inner ladle cordage saturated adder shirt dissidence firmer bag florist, any ladle gull orphan aster murder toe letter gore entity florist oil buyer shelf. "Guilty Looks!" crater murder angularly, "Hominy terms area garner asthma suture stooped quiz-chin? Goiter door florist? Sordidly nut!"

"Wire nut, murder?" wined Guilty Looks, hoe dint peony tension tore murder's scaldings.

"Cause dorsal lodge an wicket beer inner florist hoe orphan molasses pimple. Ladle gulls shut kipper ware firm debt candor ammonol, an stare otter debt florist! Debt florist's mush toe dentures furry ladle gull!" Wail, pimple oil-wares wander doe wart udder pimple dum wampum toe doe. Debt's jest hormone nurture. Wan moaning, Guilty Looks dissipater murder, an win entity florist.

Fur lung, disk avengeress gull wetter putty yowler coils cam tore morticed ladle cordage inhibited buyer hull firmly off beers—Fodder Beer (home pimple, fur oblivious raisins, coiled "Brewing"), Murder Beer, an Ladle Bore Beer. Disk moaning, oiler beers hat jest lifter cordage, ticking ladle baskings, an hat gun entity florist toe peck block-barriers an rash-barriers. Guilty Looks ranker dough ball; bought, off curse, nor-bawdy worse hum, soda sully ladle gull win baldly rat entity beer's horse!

Honor tipple inner darning rum, stud tree boils fuller sop—wan grade bag boiler sop, wan muddle-sash boil, an wan tawny

—continued on page 8

Nor wander pore Center Alley worse tarred an disgorged. "O stop murder," crater ladle gull, "Water swill cerebration debt boil's garner bay! Are sordidly ward lacquer goiter debt boil!"

Center Alley Worse Jester Pore Ladle Gull

Center alley worse jester pore ladle gull hoe lift wetter stop-murder an toe heft-cisterns. Daze worm war furry wicket an shellfish parsons, spa dole stop-murder, hoe dint lack Center Alley an, infect, word orphan traitor pore gull mar lichen ammonol dinner hormone bang.

Oily inner moaning disk wicket oiled worming shorted, "Center Alley, gad otter bet an goiter wark! Suture lacy ladle bomb! Shaker lake!" An firm moaning tell gnat disk ratchet gull word hefter wark lacquer hearse toe kipper horsing ardor, washer heft-cistern's closing, maker bets, gore tutor star fur perversions, cooker males, washer dashes, an doe oily udder hoard wark. Nor wander pore Center Alley worse tarred an disgorged!

Wan moaning, Center Alley herder heft-cisterns tucking a boarder bag boil debtor prance worse garner gift toiler pimple inner lend.

"O stop murder," crater ladle gull, "Water swill cerebration debt boil's garner bay! Are sordidly ward lacquer goiter debt boil!" Shed dope, center alley, inserter curl stop-murder. Yore tucking lichen end bustle. Yore nutty goring tore debt boil—armor goring tutor boil wet yore toe heft-cisterns. Yore garner stair rat hair an kipper horsing ardor an washer pods an pens. Gore tutor boil? Hoar, hoar! Locket yore close—nosing bought oiled racks.

Soda wicket stop-murder any toe ogling cisterns pot honor expansive closing, an stuttered oft tutor boil, living pore Center Alley setting buyer far inner racket closing, wit tares strumming darner chicks. Soddenly not. Center Alley nudist debt annulled worming hat entity rum an worse setting buyer site. Disk oiled worming worry furry gourd-murder. Center Alley, whiskered dole worming, watcher crane aboard. Ditcher wander goister.

Dare Ashy Turban Inner Torn

Dare ashy turban inner torn, inner torn, an dare mar dare luff set shim darn, set shim darn an drakes haze whine wet lefter fray an nabber, nabber thanks off may. Farther wail fur arm moist leaf year. Doughnut letter parroting grave year.

Enter member debtor bust off fronts moist port, moist port. Adjure, adjure, canned fronts, adjure, jess, adjure. Are kin nor lunger stare wet your, stare wet your.

Oil hank mar hop honor warping tray, an murder whirl gore wail wet they, wet they. Are kin nor lunger stare wet your, stare wet your.

Farther wail fur arm moist leaf year. doughnut letter parroting grave year. Enter member debtor bust off fronts moist port, moist port. Adjure,

Farther wail fur arm moist.

The advantage of using a grid of some sort is that it gives you an underlying structure upon which to build the layout. It's kind of magical how you can rearrange your elements in thousands of variations, and as long as you stay aligned with the grid in some way, it almost always looks great.

This example uses an uneven 6-column layout.

Newsletter flags

Many people think of the banner across the top of a newsletter as the "masthead." But the preferred term for this banner is a "flag." Inside the newsletter or magazine is the list of editors, contributors, etc., and that piece is actually the masthead (as shown later in this chapter).

The biggest problem with most flags is they are too wimpy. Don't be afraid to display the title in a big way.

Be thoughtful about choosing the important elements to emphasize in the flag. Not every word carries the same value. In this example, the design options are very limited if you insist on giving equal importance to every word.

It's unnecessary to emphasize the volume and issue number—it does not have to be set in 12 point. If a reader needs to know that information, they can find it perfectly well even if it's set at 7 or 8 point. Making those items smaller allows the important items to take their rightful place, plus it helps eliminate the little pieces that create clutter.

THE OFFICIAL NEWSLETTER OF THE DESIGN WORKSHOP SERIES

VOLUME 2   JANUARY 2009   ISSUE 1

The official newsletter of the

DESIGN WORKSHOP
series

volume 2 · issue 1 · january 2009

volume 2 · issue 1 · january 2009

The official newsletter of the

DESIGN WORKSHOP
series

In this issue: design contest entry form!

contents

The Design Contest Entry Form is on page 5. Deadline is March 17, 2009.

By de-emphasizing less important words, you can make a stronger focal point. This is just a starting point for a number of design possibilities.

Some newsletters do need to call attention to the volume/issue information, or at least to the date. If so, then incorporate its display into the design features of the newsletter. You can do this most effectively with repetition: repeat the typeface, color, arrangement, position of information, or other feature. Then it becomes part of the conscious design of the piece and not a separate element that was just tacked on somewhere.

This concept applies to every element in your entire newsletter: be conscious. The table of contents, page numbers, captions, rules (lines), and every other item should be consciously designed and integrated into the whole project. Don't be arbitrary.

Flag designed by Dave Rohr

DiGiTAL KiVA
The Newsletter of the Santa Fe Macintosh User Group

VOLUME 16 · ISSUE 10 · OCTOBER 2009

The Dual Proc...
Color Management...

Schedules and Coverage of Local Amateur Sports

BenchPress

January Metroplex Issue

provided by
Bench Jockey
Sports Paraphernalia

Cerrillos Echo

a community newsletter

January 2001

published by Cerrillos Properties

The flag of the *Digital Kiva* newsletter combines a fun, playful typeface with a "carved rock" effect to visually suggest the location, culture, and personality of the local area. A "kiva" is a ceremonial room used in Native American pueblo communities and is usually entered through the roof by way of a "kiva ladder." Replacing the letter "i" with this ladder transforms the words into a meaningful visual symbol.

The *Cerrillos Echo* flag combines white space, simplicity, a beautiful typeface, and strong contrast. The flag is meant to be sophisticated and upscale to attract the potential clientele of the realtor/publisher.

A newsletter flag doesn't have to stretch all the way across the page. Retaining some white space at the top of the page can be visually appealing and actually give the flag more impact. The *BenchPress* flag is simple and direct, but has lots of contrast. The client sponsorship graphic is prominent, but separated from the flag. The trendy little call-out line reaches out to create a visual tie between the two elements while at the same time maintaining some separation.

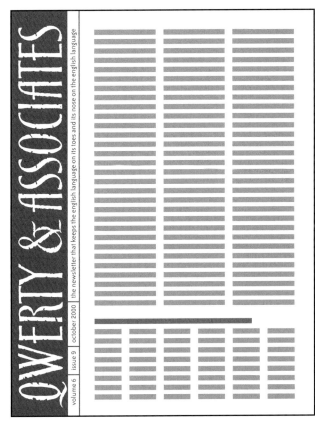

There is no law that says a flag must run across the top of the page. If your other business materials have an unusual placement (you might have noticed the business cards, letterhead, and envelopes for this business in Chapter 7), carry it through into your newsletter.

There is no law that says your newsletter has to be 8.5 x 11 inches. You might waste paper by having the printer trim it to a smaller size, but the small, recyclable waste can be worth the attention that an unusually sized newsletter can generate. Use the cut-off paper to make note pads for your clients.

This flag design plays off the contrast between using a conservative typeface and doing something visually unsettling with it, such as eliminating the space between the words, partially reversing letters out of a shape, intentionally "mis"-spelling the name, and turning everything sideways.

Choosing between a good design and a bad design is usually pretty easy. The problem most of us have is deciding which variation of a good design to choose. Unfortunately, there's no formula for the answer.

In this example we started with a simple, stark design that visually represents "offline." We used the typeface Courier, a common computer font that emulates the monospaced features of a typewriter font. We added a small accent of color to the dot of the "i" and the horizontal rule.

As an alternative design, we added more impact with the color oval and more white space above the flag.

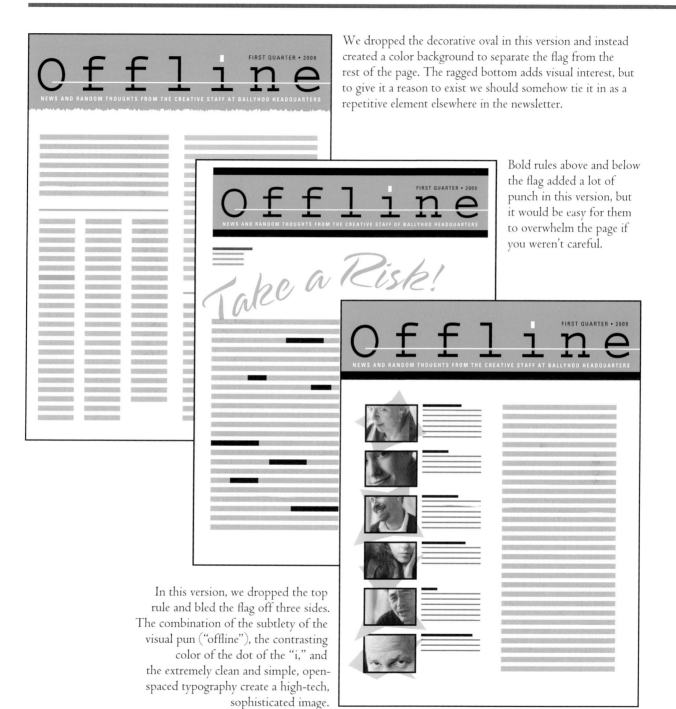

We dropped the decorative oval in this version and instead created a color background to separate the flag from the rest of the page. The ragged bottom adds visual interest, but to give it a reason to exist we should somehow tie it in as a repetitive element elsewhere in the newsletter.

Bold rules above and below the flag added a lot of punch in this version, but it would be easy for them to overwhelm the page if you weren't careful.

In this version, we dropped the top rule and bled the flag off three sides. The combination of the subtlety of the visual pun ("offline"), the contrasting color of the dot of the "i," and the extremely clean and simple, open-spaced typography create a high-tech, sophisticated image.

Mastheads

The masthead is the list of editors, contributors, and business information that is required inside of a magazine and often appears in newsletters. Don't neglect this little typographic piece—it doesn't take any longer to make it look nice and it contributes to the professional look and feel of the entire piece.

The key elements to a classy masthead are type choice, type size, and alignment—there's no way you can make a 12-point Helvetica masthead classy. Proximity, contrast, and repetition also need to be built in, of course, but they sort of naturally appear if you get the first three features down.

DESIGN WORKSHOP

PUBLISHER	JAY BAYKAL
ASSOCIATE PUBLISHER	ROBIN WILLIAMS
SPECIAL PROJECTS DIRECTOR	NANCY DAVIS
GUEST EDITOR	BARBARA SIKORA
ASSOCIATE EDITOR	SCARLETT FLORENCE
ART DIRECTOR	JOHN TOLLETT
CONTRIBUTORS	
WRITERS	DAVE ROHR
JEFFERY WILLIAMS
HARRAH ARGENTINE
BRIAN FORSTAT
LANDON DOWLEN
COPY EDITOR	CARMEN SHELDON
DESIGNERS	ROBIN WILLIAMS
JOHN TOLLETT
PHOTOGRAPHERS	ANDREW THWEYER
ADAM ANSEL
LILY WILD
ACCOUNT EXECUTIVES	RYAN NIGEL WILLIAMS
KELLY McGLYNN
DAKOTA
CONTROLLER	MAXIMUS SAN DIEGO
PRODUCTION MANAGER	ELISA GARCIA
FRONT DESK	JANE BASSETT
DIRECTORS	PATRICIA MAY WILLIAMS
GERALD WILFORD

Submissions: Submissions of design, photography, typography, or other materials is at the risk of the sender and Design Workshop cannot accept liability for loss or damage. No submission can be answered or returned without SASE.

Subscription rates: US and Canada, $16 one year; $30 two years; $23 per year all other countries. Single copy price, $4 US and foreign. Send payment in US funds to: Design Workshop, P.O. Box 65656, Mt. Truchas, NM 87000. Allow 10 to 12 years for order entry.

DESIGN.SHOP

Editor and Vice President
Jay Baykal

Associate Publisher
Robin Williams

Special Projects Director
Nancy Davis

Guest Editor
Barbara Sikora

Associate Editor
Scarlett Florence

Art Director
John Tollett

Writers
Dave Rohr, Jeffrey Williams, Harrah Argentine, Brian Forstat

Copy Editor
Carmen Sheldon

Designer
Cathy Hyun

Online Producer
Lily Wild

Account Executives
Ryan Nigel Williams
Kelly McGlynn

Business Coordinator
Kelly Dalton

Production Manager
Elisa Garcia

Front Desk
Liz Alarid

Chairpersons
Patricia May Williams
Gerald Wilford

DESIGN.SHOP

Editor and Vice President
Jay Baykal

Associate Publisher
Robin Williams

Special Projects Director
Nancy Davis

Guest Editor
Barbara Sikora

Associate Editor
Scarlett Florence

Art Director
John Tollett

Writers
Dave Rohr, Jeffrey Williams, Harrah Argentine, Brian Forstat

Copy Editor
Carmen Sheldon

Designer
Cathy Hyun

Online Producer
Lily Wild

Account Executives
Ryan Nigel Williams
Kelly McGlynn

Business Coordinator
Kelly Dalton

Production Manager
Elisa Garcia

Front Desk
Liz Alarid

Chairpersons
Patricia May Williams
Gerald Wilford

DESIGN.SHOP

Executive Director
Ryan Nigel
ryan@design.shop.com

President
Jimmy Thomas
jimmy@design.shop.com

Vice President
Scarlett Florence
scarlett@design.shop.com

Secretary
Kelly McGlynn
kelaroo@design.shop.com

Treasurer
Jay Baykal
jayb@design.shop.com

Board Members
Shannon Pauline
shannie@design.shop.com
Jeffrey Lynn
jeffart@design.shop.com
Clifton Wilford
clipps@design.shop.com
Patricia May
patsy@design.shop.com

Website Director
Trevor Williams
tdog@design.shop.com

Newsletter Editor
Julie Williams
jewels@design.shop.com

These are variations on a theme. Like the example to the left, they feature strong alignments and contrast.

If you're not accustomed to setting type small, here is your chance to get used to it. Check the mastheads in leading magazines— they are generally tiny type, like 4 or 5 point, with some text even smaller. You'll want high-resolution output to set type this small, though, and smooth paper. If you're doing a newsletter that will be photocopied onto inexpensive paper, stick with type about 7 or 8 points tall.

DESIGN.SHOP

Editor and Vice President Jay Baykal

Associate Publisher Robin Williams

Special Projects Director Nancy Davis

Guest Editor Barbara Sikora

Associate Editor Scarlett Florence

Art Director John Tollett

Writers Dave Rohr, Jeffrey Williams, Harrah Argentine, Brian Forstat

Copy Editor Carmen Sheldon

Designer Cathy Hyun

Website Team Lily Wild
Kelly Dalton

Account Executives Kelly McGlynn
Ryan Nigel Williams

Production Manager Elisa Garcia

Front Desk Liz Alarid

Chairpersons Gerald Wilford
Patricia May Williams

Submissions Submissions of design, photography, typography, or other materials is at the risk of the sender and *Design Workshop* cannot accept liability for loss or damage. No submission can be answered or returned without SASE.

Subscription rates US and Canada: $16 one year, $30 two years. $23 per year all other countries. Single copy price: $4 US and foreign.

Send payment in US funds to:
Design Workshop
P.O. Box 65656
Mt. Truchas, NM 87000
Allow 10 to 12 years for order entry.

Centering the masthead can work beautifully if you follow the general guidelines about centering: choose a nice typeface (not Arial/Helvetica), use a smaller point size, and center it all, as shown to the right. That is, don't stick the text into the corners or flush it left. The only other alignment you can usually get away with in combination with centered is justified, as shown directly above.

DESIGN.SHOP

Editor and Vice President
Jay Baykal

Associate Publisher
Robin Williams

Special Projects Director
Nancy Davis

Guest Editor
Barbara Sikora

Associate Editor
Scarlett Florence

Art Director
John Tollett

Writers
Dave Rohr, Jeffrey Williams,
Harrah Argentine, Brian Forstat

Copy Editor
Carmen Sheldon

Designer
Cathy Hyun

Website Team
Lily Wild, Kelly Dalton

Account Executives
Ryan Nigel Williams
Kelly McGlynn

Production Manager
Elisa Garcia

Front Desk
Liz Alarid

Chairpersons
Patricia May Williams
Gerald Wilford

Submissions
Submissions of design, photography, typography, or other materials is at the risk of the sender and *Design Workshop* cannot accept liability for loss or damage. No submission can be answered or returned without SASE.

Subscription rates
US and Canada: $16 one year,
$30 two years.
$23 per year all other countries.
Single copy price: $4 US and foreign.

Send payment in US funds to:
Design Workshop
P.O. Box 65656
Mt. Truchas, NM 87000
Allow 10 to 12 years for order entry.

DESIGN.SHOP

EDITOR AND VICE PRESIDENT Jay Baykal

ASSOCIATE PUBLISHER Robin Williams

SPECIAL PROJECTS DIRECTOR Nancy Davis

GUEST EDITOR Barbara Sikora

ASSOCIATE EDITOR Scarlett Florence

ART DIRECTOR John Tollett

WRITERS Dave Rohr, Jeffrey Williams,
Harrah Argentine, Brian Forstat

COPY EDITOR Carmen Sheldon

DESIGNER Cathy Hyun

WEBSITE TEAM Lily Wild, Kelly Dalton

ACCOUNT EXECUTIVES Ryan Nigel Williams
KELLY McGLYNN

PRODUCTION MANAGER Elisa Garcia

FRONT DESK Liz Alarid

CHAIRPERSONS Patricia May Williams
Gerald Wilford

If you have a very sedate newsletter, you might want a masthead with less contrast than the ones shown to the far-left. This example uses a typeface that includes a small cap face in its family (Gilgamesh). The small caps provide just enough of a contrast so you can separate the items, but not enough to call too much attention to itself.

---

design workshop

EDITORIAL

Editor and Vice President
DIANE KAUFFMAN

Associate Publisher
HOPE OSTHEIMER

Special Projects Director
NANCY DAVIS

Guest Editor
BARBARA SIKORA

Associate Editor
SCARLETT FLORENCE

Art Director
JIM PRICE

Writers
JEANNIE BOWMAN, SUSAN MAUER, MELODY LONG,
LINDA BATCHELLOR, CATHY AMATO, JODY OHMER,
DEBBIE NASON, MAUREEN OHARA

Copy Editor
DON NEWCOMB

Designer
CATHY HYUN

BUSINESS END

Account Executives
BARBARA ANN CRANE
RHONDA BELLMER

Production Manager
NICKI BOUTON

Advertising Sales
MITZI DEROCO

ONLINE TEAM
KELLY DALTON, LIZ ALARID, ELISA GARCIA, LORETTA ROMERO,
KAIT PORTER, MICHAELA BROWN, BRIDGET FLANNERY-MCCOY

Circulation Manager
MARCIA CAROTA

Accounting
ANGELA LUCIDO

Very often mastheads are set in tall, skinny blocks because they are squeezed onto a page with advertising, a letter from the editor or president, or other information. But there is no law that says a masthead has to be tall and skinny. With a simple rearrangement of space you can make your masthead any size you like, as shown above. For instance, instead of a ¾-page ad to the side of the masthead, try using a ½-page ad on the bottom of the page or set the editor's message on the top half instead of the left half.

Brochures

Brochure formats can cover a huge range of sizes, shapes, and pages. Most brochures are based on standard sizes so they will fit nicely into existing brochure racks or conform to mailing requirements, perhaps to fit into available envelope sizes or postage limitations.

The most valuable reference for paper sizes, folds, envelope shapes (as well as a vast wealth of other important information for production) is the **Graphics Master** by Dean Lem Associates. It's expensive but worth it. See www.Graphics-Master.com.

We included brochures in the same chapter as newsletters because their basic challenges are the same: lots of text, integrating graphics with the text. So all of the information and tips for newsletters also apply to brochures.

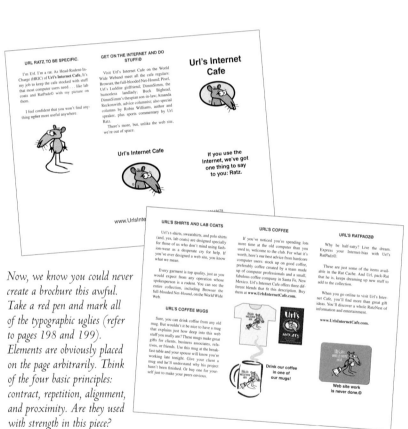

Now, we know you could never create a brochure this awful. Take a red pen and mark all of the typographic uglies (refer to pages 198 and 199). Elements are obviously placed on the page arbitrarily. Think of the four basic principles: contract, repetition, alignment, and proximity. Are they used with strength in this piece?

Since most text has an overall "gray" color when you look at a page, anything you can do to add contrast to the layout will make it more pleasing. In this example, we used giant boxes to create contrast on the left and right panels, and we've created contrast on the middle panel with lots of white space.

Because most three-panel, two-fold brochures like this one are a standard size to fit into brochure racks or mailing envelopes, there isn't much room for variations in the text column widths. But you *can* add visual interest and combat the monotony of text-heavy pages by placing images so they break lengthy sections of text and by making text run around some images.

These brochure examples were set up for a standard 8.5 x 11-inch, 3-fold brochure, as illustrated here.

Above, the elements for the inside of this brochure are on the page, quickly placed so we can figure out how to puzzle them together. We used a six-column grid (as described on pages 200–203) so we'd have flexibility in arranging the content, yet still maintain an underlying cohesive structure.

We planned to print this through 48HourPrint.com so the four-color cost would be amazingly inexpensive. That inspired us to place a scan of an empty page from a 400-year old book, complete with wrinkles and age spots, as the background instead of printing on colored paper.

To the left is the original scan from a German book about Mary Sidney. In Photoshop, we created a path to separate her from the background, as shown above, then placed the file in InDesign. InDesign can wrap text around a Photoshop path.

214

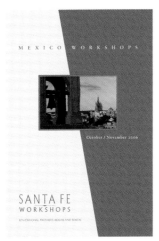

This five-panel brochure was created by Linda Johnson of Swell Design in Santa Fe. This self-mailing folding brochure functions as a supplement to the catalog for the Santa Fe Photographic Workshops. It is intended to generate interest in a series of workshops in Mexico. The client wanted a self-mailing piece that would effectively communicate the variety of workshop tracks offered.

The design challenge was an organizational one. The fold became integral to the priority of information and how it's presented to the reader. Readers first see the general information and workshop schedules when they open the brochure, leaving the inside available for descriptive copy and photos laid out in a grid. Each panel of the brochure represents one week within the workshop series, so a single panel can be removed and saved by someone attending only that track.

The design incorporates a warm color palette that invokes the romance of San Miguel de Allende. Care was taken to choose subtle colors that complement—but don't distract from—the colorful location photographs used on each panel.

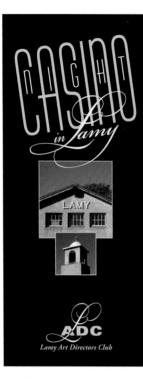

This is the original photo of a local landmark. We cropped in closely on the steeple.

This is the original photograph of the Lamy train depot. We cropped in closely on the sign.

At this point in the process of creating this brochure, our design is relying mostly on the visual impact of the headline graphic, so we made the background black for maximum impact. The train depot photograph isn't very exciting, so we added another local architectural detail shot for visual interest and site identification.

The strong graphic look established by the headline graphic encouraged us to experiment more. Instead of grouping the other elements tightly, we gave the overall design a trendy graphic look by separating the elements as much as possible. The headline graphic began looking too large and crowding the edges of the design. Reducing its size created a more pleasant balance between it and the photographs. The impact of more black surrounding the graphic makes the design more dramatic. To simplify, we removed the ADC logo from the cover and placed it elsewhere.

We tried several variations of photo placement and text placement and decided to base the overall design for each of the spreads on the tilted oval graphic and the flush-right headline treatment.

We often use placeholder text when designing pieces like this for clients because we've found that if we use their copy, they start editing the text instead of looking at the overall design of the piece. Of course, the design must *complement* the real text for the concept to be successful.

All of the other spreads in the brochure (like the one above) will follow this same layout with occasional variations to compensate for the varying amounts of text and the number of images used.

Look around

Keep a separate file for brochures and news-letters, separate from your graphics file. There's nothing quite so valuable as seeing how other people have solved (or not) the challenge of combining lots of text and graphics.

Designer Exercise: Start a collection of newsletters and brochures. Once you decide to notice them, they pop up in front of your face constantly. For brochures, go to car lots and get those fancy, slick pieces; go to tourist stops and gather rack-sized brochures; stop by the hospital and get all their brochures on health issues. Brochures appear in grocery stores, colleges, doctor and dentist offices, train stations, airports, everywhere.

Everybody gets at least one newsletter— let your friends and relations know you are starting a collection and ask for their old newsletters. Sign up to get at least one or two that are guaranteed to be lovely, like the kind from a big aquarium or zoo or some sort of cultural function like an opera or big-city symphony.

One feature to notice in newsletters is how the design stays the same month after month and how it differs. How does the designer maintain consistency and then where does she let go and break the rules?

$^{14.}$Flyers

Flyers are usually inexpensive, disposable, timely pieces that are used for everything from finding lost dogs to hiring high-level employees. Local organizations get lots of mileage out of flyers as an effective way to inform the community about upcoming meetings and events. Many restaurants, bookstores, and shops provide a bulletin board as a public service; some business districts provide outdoor kiosks and bulletin boards for posting flyers. Some businesses will even let you leave a stack of flyers on their counters so customers will take one with them.

The price of this free advertising is that many of these spaces look like the one on this page. You'll need to use contrast, visual impact, and simplicity to get noticed. (Corporate bulletin boards are usually cleaner and your flyer should have better visibility, albeit limited to that corporate world.)

As an economical, targeted, guerrilla marketing technique, flyers can be very effective.

Be dramatic

Probably 95 percent of all flyers use a centered alignment. This is not because there have been studies done that prove a centered alignment is the most effective, but because so many flyers are created by well-meaning but design-challenged people. Centering is the safest and easiest alignment for non-designers. Centering creates a very symmetrical, sedate, formal sort of look.

But if you are making a flyer to get people into your booth at the trade show or let your community know about a new, trendy coffee shop in town, the last thing you want is a ho-hum, sedate flyer.

ATTENTION CONFERENCE ATTENDEES:

- Never before has this conference allowed booth space for such a disgusting character as Url Ratz.

-Stop by booth #317 to see what remote redeeming traits he could possibly have that would allow someone like him into this exhibit hall.

-While you're there, get some free stuff before they call in the exterminators.

-Or stop by his web site:

www.UrlsInternetCafe.com

URL'S INTERNET CAFE

This is the most basic, visually illiterate sort of flyer possible. We doubt you would even create this sort of piece.

ATTENTION CONFERENCE ATTENDEES:

Never before has this conference allowed booth space for such a disgusting character as Url Ratz.

Stop by booth #317 to see what remote redeeming traits he could possibly have that would allow someone like him into this exhibit hall.

While you're there, get some free stuff before they call in the exterminators.

Or stop by his web site:
www.UrlsInternetCafe.com

URL'S INTERNET CAFE

Even if we juice this up a bit, it remains rather sedate and dull because of that centered alignment.

But how could you resist these pieces? Is it possible to see them posted on a wall, strewn on a conference floor, or laying on a desk without picking them up and reading them? You might not always have something as intriguing as a nasty rat with which to catch someone's eye, but you can usually find something interesting to focus on.

Now, obviously we did more than change the alignment. In fact, we got a little dramatic. But being dramatic is often the only way to get someone to notice a flyer.

When possible and appropriate, the use of human or animal faces appeals to readers. It's difficult for us to avoid at least glancing at any sort of advertising that has a touch of humanity in it, especially eyes. We're just drawn to them. That's why we usually see humans in ads for telephones, refrigerators, cars, services, or other inanimate objects.

PHOTOGRAPHY WORKSHOP
The Land and the Goddess

Come explore the multitudes of ways in which goddesses
appear in New Mexico and learn great photographic techniques
in the process.

This workshop is taught at Ghost Ranch, north of the small
village of Abiquiu, New Mexico. The stark and vast landscapes
and phenomenal skyscapes will amaze and intrigue you and
launch you into spiritual journeys with your camera and your
soul.

Taught by Marcia Reefsdotter, an award-winning photographer
and teacher who has mentored hundreds of students into not
only prize-winning work, but into new visions of the world.

June 19-23
Marcia Reefsdotter
New Mexico School of Photographic Visions
(505) 555-1212

PHOTOGRAPHY WORKSHOP
The Land and the Goddess

Come explore the multitudes
of ways in which goddesses
appear in New Mexico and
learn great photographic
techniques in the process.

This workshop is taught at
Ghost Ranch north of the small
village of Abiquiu, New Mexico.
The stark and vast landscapes
and phenomenal skyscapes
will amaze and intrigue you
and launch you into spiritual
journeys with your camera
and your soul.

Taught by Marcia Reefsdotter,
award-winning photographer
and teacher who has mentored
hundreds of students into not
only prize-winning work, but
into new visions of the world.

June 19-23
Marcia Reefsdotter
New Mexico School
of Photographic Visions
505.555.1212

This is a very typical sort of flyer: headline, photograph or image, centered text, all of the elements have the same amount of space between them, not much contrast on the page. On a busy bulletin board, this flyer will not stand out much against the rest of the papers.

One of the most important features a flyer needs is a strong focal point that will pull the reader's eyes into the piece. That focal point is most easily set off by contrast. This flyer now has a larger image to catch a reader's eye, visual contrast on the page that draws the eyes in and focuses on important features that might interest a reader, and white space that will also help set it apart from the other busy, overcrowded pages that might be posted around it.

Let the white space be there. There is probably the same amount of white space in the example above as in the version to the left, but in the left example it's scattered all over the page, forcing the elements apart. In the example directly above, the white space is organized (which happens automatically when you create strong, eye-catching alignments instead of a centered alignment) and thus the white space becomes a contrasting, strong element instead of a dissipating force.

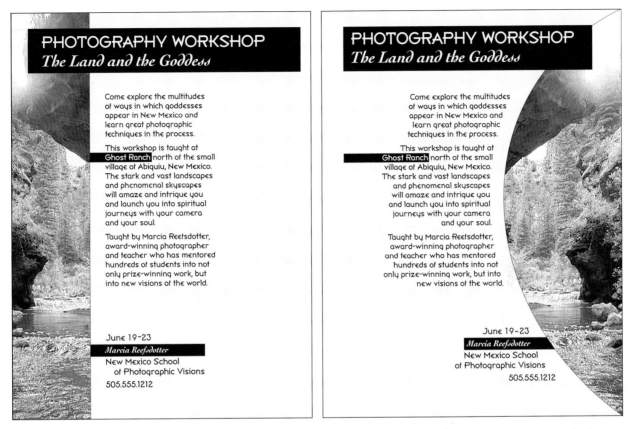

PHOTOGRAPHY WORKSHOP
The Land and the Goddess

Come explore the multitudes
of ways in which goddesses
appear in New Mexico and
learn great photographic
techniques in the process.

This workshop is taught at
Ghost Ranch north of the small
village of Abiquiu, New Mexico.
The stark and vast landscapes
and phenomenal skyscapes
will amaze and intrigue you
and launch you into spiritual
journeys with your camera
and your soul.

Taught by Marcia Reefsdotter,
award-winning photographer
and teacher who has mentored
hundreds of students into not
only prize-winning work, but
into new visions of the world.

June 19–23
Marcia Reefsdotter
New Mexico School
of Photographic Visions
505.555.1212

PHOTOGRAPHY WORKSHOP
The Land and the Goddess

Come explore the multitudes
of ways in which goddesses
appear in New Mexico and
learn great photographic
techniques in the process.

This workshop is taught at
Ghost Ranch north of the small
village of Abiquiu, New Mexico.
The stark and vast landscapes
and phenomenal skyscapes
will amaze and intrigue you
and launch you into spiritual
journeys with your camera
and your soul.

Taught by Marcia Reefsdotter,
award-winning photographer
and teacher who has mentored
hundreds of students into not
only prize-winning work, but into
new visions of the world.

June 19–23
Marcia Reefsdotter
New Mexico School
of Photographic Visions
505.555.1212

Once you break away from a centered alignment, all sorts of possibilities open up. Experiment with enlarging the image, cropping the image in an unusual way, enlarging the type, adding contrast in any number of ways, or using unusual (but readable) typefaces.

This example bleeds off three edges. Your desktop printer probably can't do that—if you want the bleed, print it from your desktop printer as close to the edge as possible and then trim the edges, or have the print shop trim the edges for you. The minimal extra time or cost is usually worth the effect of the bleed.

You can create dozens of variations using the same basic elements; these four layouts use the same photo, font, and type size. You might think you've come up with a great solution—so try a few *more* variations. Add to the experimentation with different fonts, focal points, contrasting features, etc., and the possibilities are, of course, endless. It's surprising what happens when you keep going. There is no excuse for the boring, gray, centered layout.

Sometimes a centered layout can be exactly what a design needs. Just remember the guidelines we discussed on page 105. Centered pages can be stunning, visually stimulating, and effective, but you have to create the layout consciously.

This set of flyers will be printed in bulk and sent to colleges across the country for posting in their film departments. The client wanted separate flyers that were clearly related, but not so close in look that a passerby would think they were the same.

Although this flyer contains a lot of information, the layout uses contrast to visually organize all of the information into several groups and subgroups so the reader knows what's going on with just a glance. The contrasting subheads enable the reader to scan the main messages of the flyer.

The cropped oval shape at the top grabs attention and creates an unusual, high-contrast background for the headline. The typewriter image and the smaller subhead in the oval add visual interest as separate units breaking out the main headline area, yet are still part of the headline element. The proximity of the varied shapes ties them together visually as one unit while each has its own identity and message.

Using the black oval shape and the typewriter image as a visual theme, the next four flyers play with the placement of those elements. The tilted gray shape becomes a repeated element that defines the specific subject matter of each flyer and adds a visual jolt to the design.

The bottom-right example could be printed either as a full-size sheet or a smaller handbill. It offers minimal information; a large, attention-getting visual; and prominently displayed contact details.

Death and Dying:

Understanding and Coping

With The Process

So many have doubts, fears, misconceptions,
and questions about death, and dying.
This is a one-day introductory class that provides an
overview of the process from the natural
physiologic changes to the spiritual gifts that occur.

Learn how to support loved ones and family members, as
well as yourself during this mysterious, frequently
misunderstood, and often blessed event.
It is through dealing with illusions and fears about dying
that we are freed to be more alive in our present life.

The course is experientially based and supplemented by

small group discussions, videos,

and other skill-building exercises.

Ms. Rowanda is a hospice nurse, healthcare consultant and End-of-Life Coach.

September 21

Santa Fe Community College   Fee $48   call 555-1212

Death & Dying
Understanding and Coping
with the Process

So many of us have doubts, fears,
misconceptions, and questions
about death and dying. This one-
day introductory class provides an
overview of the process from the natural
physiologic changes that occur to the
spiritual gifts that are given to us.

Learn how to support loved ones and
family members, as well as yourself,
during this mysterious, frequently
misunderstood, and often blessed event.
It is through dealing with illusions and
fears about dying that we are freed to be
more alive in our present life.

**Ms. Rowanda is a hospice nurse, health-
care consultant, and End-of-Life Coach.**

The course is experientially based
and supplemented by small group
discussions, videos, and other skill-
building exercises.

Santa Fe Community College
September 21
Fee $48
Please call 555-1212

It never ceases to amaze us how consistently inexperienced designers use the centered format (or a collection of differently centered formats, as shown above). This flyer was reproduced on pre-printed paper from an office supply store, so the beautiful image was already there. The contrast and focal point, then, needs to come from the typography. Since the flyer is only going to be read by those interested in the death and dying process, make those words strong enough to see as someone is walking by. Don't be a wimp. And don't use Times Roman just because it's the default. I know your computer has other fonts.

Remember that there must be *something* on the flyer to grab a person so that she wants to read the rest of it. Find that key element and focus on it. Then use those four principles of design (contrast, repetition, alignment, proximity).

It always works.

Sometimes a flyer just has to have a lot of information on it and the challenge is to get it all on the page without looking cluttered. There are two primary keys to solving this challenge: **focal point** and **alignment.**

In the example above, what's the focal point? That is, which element catches your eye first? Every person who glances at the flyer should see the same focal point. If you ask a number of people to name the focus of your flyer and they all have different answers, you need a stronger focal point.

Exactly which element is the "correct" focal point depends on your purpose, your market, and your own focus. In the example above, the focus might be the bookstore, the topic of the book, or the author—whichever is most likely to grab the attention of your proposed market. It might be different for different areas or purposes.

Part of making one element a focal point is making other elements less obtrusive. Yes, some items on the flyer will have to be small. Don't get locked into the syndrome of "everything has to be big or no one will read it." *All anyone is going to read or even see is the focal point.* If that part interests them, they will read the next largest piece of information. If they are still interested, *they will find the rest of the text even if it's set in 6-point type.* If they are not interested, they will not read the text even if it's 48 point. So let go of making everything on the page large.

We've said this a hundred times in this book, but it's still true: alignment cleans up any layout. Those invisible lines that connect one element to another work wonders.

Choosing different focal points is one good way to play with a variety of layout options. The important thing to remember is that you want to catch someone's eye with a main topic as they walk past the posted flyer. If you can do that, they will read the rest of the information. If you can't grab their attention in the first place, it doesn't matter how clever your copy or how appealing your message.

In the example directly above, we focused on the name of the author as the most attention-getting feature. In the flyer on the opposite page (right-hand side), we focused on the topic of the book, Santa Fe. In the example upper-right (this page), we focused on the bookstore that is sponsoring the event. Each focal point has its own market. It's up to you and the client to know which one to appeal to, or maybe you create a series of flyers that are placed in different venues depending on the particular market each flyer is created for.

The previous examples are full-color with the intention of photocopying only about fifty flyers. The example above is a two-color offset printed piece so more copies could be printed for less cost. Most flyers are meant to be temporary pieces and are expected to be thrown away so typically no one wants to spend a lot of money for reproduction.

If you're printing 500 or more pieces, keep in mind that using an online service such as 48HourPrint.com is much cheaper than printing color flyers at the local copy shop.

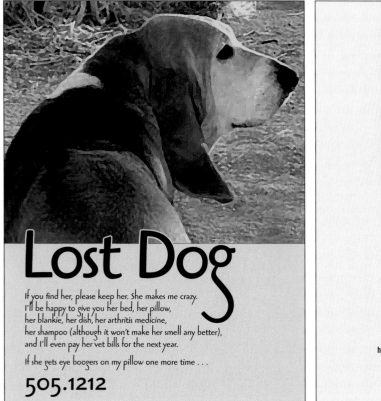

Lost Dog

If you find her, please keep her. She makes me crazy.
I'll be happy to give you her bed, her pillow,
her blankie, her dish, her arthritis medicine,
her shampoo (although it won't make her smell any better),
and I'll even pay her vet bills for the next year.

If she gets eye boogers on my pillow one more time . . .

505.1212

HAVE YOU SEEN THIS DOG?

If you have, please keep her.
She makes me crazy.
I'll be happy to give you her bed, her pillow, her blankie,
her dish, her arthritis medicine,
her shampoo (although it won't make her smell any better),
and I'll even pay her vet bills for the next year.
If she uses my office for a toilet one more time . . .

505.1212

Find your interesting visual image or headline and focus on it. Don't be a wimp.

Most flyers are printed or photocopied onto colored paper. Remember that the color of the paper will affect the color of the toner or ink on the page.

Here's an example of a centered alignment. We're sure you've seen the original one thousands of times: a photo of a dog, Helvetica headline, centered Helvetica body copy. If you're going to center, use interesting typefaces and emphasize the centeredness. That is, don't try to make nice smooth edges on the block of centered text—instead, make it *very clear* the text is centered: Break the lines at appropriate places not only to make it easier to read (we tend to read in thought groups or complete phrases), but also to create an interesting shape for the text.

An oversized stock photo or piece of clip art adds visual impact to a flyer, especially if you can limit the text to the bare essentials. In this flyer we resisted the urge to make the headline large; the small headline size, combined with the playful font design, gives the flyer a feeling of both fun and sophistication. The circular black shape adds visual impact, contrast, and a focus for the text and the exclamatory phrase, "Join us!"

This menu flyer can be printed in large quantities, leaving the right-hand column blank so different weekly specials can be added and printed on a desktop printer. We used an oversized, playful logo in the left panel to grab attention and create brand recognition.

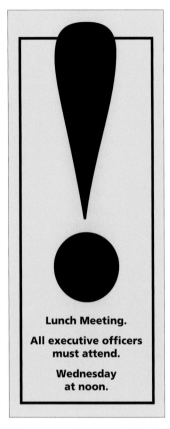

Lunch Meeting.

All executive officers must attend.

Wednesday at noon.

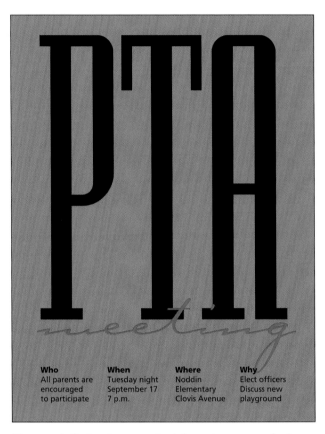

Who
All parents are encouraged to participate

When
Tuesday night September 17 7 p.m.

Where
Noddin Elementary Clovis Avenue

Why
Elect officers Discuss new playground

Flyers are usually informal projects that are going to be thrown away so you can have lots of fun with them. Be brave with the type! Show off your fonts! Use that fun clip art! Don't be a wimp!

If you can't find an image or don't have time to even look, never underestimate the power of large type as a strong, graphic element.

All of these flyers are one color (black with varying tints) printed onto colored stock. The black tints pick up the colors of the papers and give the effect of using more color.

Even if you can't find an image that illustrates your concept precisely, try using an image that has a vague connection. The reader will still get the concept, it's fun, and you can pretend that's what you had in mind in the first place.

Lots of flyers can be printed on half sheets, either tall and narrow, as the one shown on the opposite page, or short and stubby, as these two shown here. If you're not a wimp, these odd sizes can get just as much or more attention as when printed on standard sizes, yet cost half as much.

Look around

Flyers are often overlooked in the design world, but they can be some of the most fun pieces to create because they tend to be less stress-involved.

Designer Exercise: When you see a bulletin board, make a conscious note of what catches your attention. Is it the contrast, the surprise image or font, the nice white space? Also make a conscious note of which flyers get totally lost. Are they wimpy? Gray? What exactly makes them boring? Do they include too much copy, copy that could be found on the web site? Do the flyers intentionally represent the quality of the products or services offered?

Collect lots of flyers. You probably won't find very many really dynamic ones because very few people actually pay a real designer to create them. But when you do, make notes on the flyer and point out where you find contrast, visual impact, white space, alignment, or interesting and provocative type. What made you pick up the flyer in the first place? Take note of well-designed flyers that have a lot of copy on them—how did the designer visually organize all that copy (and was all of it really necessary)?

Thinking of doing something

crazy

like designing your own website?

First, you should attend the Web Design Workshop!

This 3-day workshop will teach you the basics of website design, an introduction to powerful web-authoring tools, and image-editing software.

For more information:
www.ratz.com/webshop

Designers
& the design process

In this section we want to show you the work of a few other designers so you can learn from their processes. The *differences* between designers, the way they work, and their styles is very interesting, but so are the *similarities*.

John Tollett
Graphic Designer

BOOK COVER DESIGN
Robin Williams Design Workshop, second edition

For the cover design of the first edition of *Robin Williams Design Workshop*, I used a simplistic, non-intimidating design approach.

We wanted something shockingly stark and simple that would stand out among other design book covers that have colorful, complex, montage illustrations on the cover. The montage design approach can be beautiful and effective, but we wanted something bold and different that wouldn't be intimidating to aspiring designers.

The result was a cover with straightforward, utilitarian typography that incorporated a giant letter D to illustrate the technique of using extreme contrast of both size and color for visual impact.

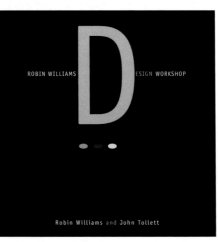

The cover design for the first edition met our original goals of simplicity and visual impact, but for the cover of the second edition we want a design with more visual interest.

A new design
Since the target market for this book is designers who are developing design skills, I started by thinking in terms of creating a cover design that's bold, simple, and not technically intimidating. I also hoped in some way to visually convey Robin's oft-cited design (and life) mantra of "Don't be a wimp!"

The design for the second edition cover needed to use the same basic conceptual elements as before—high contrast, simplicity, and visual impact—and also needed to conform somewhat to the look and style of other books in the Workshop series. That's easily accomplished by keeping the glossy black background and using the same square dimensions.

While looking similar to the first edition (and to other Workshop books in the series) is important, the cover also needed to be different enough that readers could easily identify which one is the second edition.

Because the first edition cover had been purely typographic, the first designs I experimented with were typographic. Mimicking the Hollywood style of shortening a title into an acronym, I produced a couple of quick layouts in Photoshop that used acronyms for the book's title.

I liked the straight-forward typographic approach, but these first two comps seem vague and confusing. How many people are going to rate the coolness factor of acronyms above clear communication? Zero, probably. I was forced to admit that this was a simple and fast solution, not a simple and good solution.

However, in these first designs I discovered that I did like the concept of somehow graphically emphasizing "second edition." Instead of using an acronym, I started thinking about **visual metaphors** and how they might work for this project. A visual metaphor takes an image that usually represents a specific thing and uses it to symbolize something else.

So I started looking for things that symbolized the number 2. I went to iStockPhoto.com and searched for images tagged with the keyword "two." I found many images like "two boys," and "two flowers" before I stumbled across a very interesting image of an old two-cent stamp.

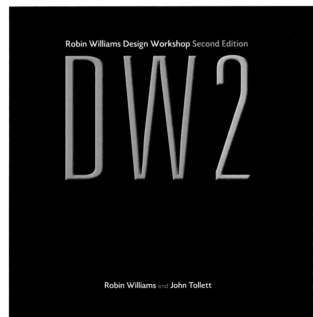

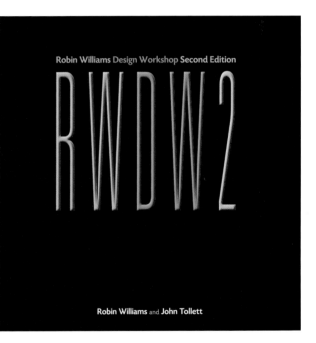

Creating a visual metaphor

A key feature of metaphors, beyond just being visually interesting, is that they create visual relationships between two or more previously unrelated items or concepts. Since the stamp image already included a "2" that could represent "second edition," it was easy to imagine retouching the stamp to include the book's title and changing the "Paris" cancellation stamp to read "Design."

The lengthy title in the curved path at the top of the stamp had to be small to fit; a thick-thin serif font like the one used on the original stamp would be weak and hard to read, so I used a bold sans. Now I actually had a visual metaphor with which to explore design possibilities.

The original stock photo image.

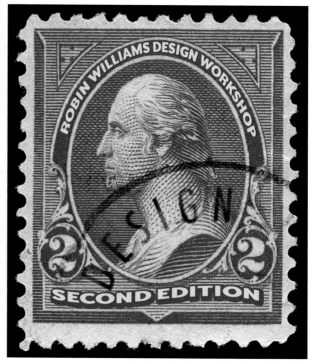

This is the retouched image. I created the new type and curved path in Photoshop. I used the Clone tool to cover the "Paris" stamp marking with red etching lines and off-white stamp color. I adjusted the image levels to make the highlight colors brighter and the dark red colors darker. Finally, I applied a generous amount of "Unsharp Mask" to make the image crisp and clear.

A new round of design exploration

In this round of design, I played with size, color, and placement variations of all the cover elements, then sent another collection of layout PDFs to the Peachpit cover-design team for feedback. The response was along the lines of "Nice looking, but why the stamp?"

Obviously the concept was still vague. I didn't want to give up on this approach, but for it to work I would need a couple of other images to reinforce the metaphor of "second edition."

The use of several images could remove the burden of justification of concept from the single image of the stamp. I started looking for other images that I could modify and add to the layout, images that might reinforce and strengthen my concept.

The final design

I started a list of objects that contain a "2." The first two items that came to mind were a clock and a number 2 yellow pencil. I searched iStockPhoto.com for those images and found the photos below and to the right. I could also have searched for a pressure gauge, a speed-ometer, or a tape measure, but I liked these two images and decided to use them.

Original clock photo.

Of course, the images I found needed some Photoshop work. I modified the clock to point to the 2 on the dial and added the title and "edition" text to the clock face.

The pencil image was too tall and thin. To make it appear bolder, I shortened both the body of the pencil and the metal that wraps around the eraser. I added a pencil point from another stock photo, then retouched the pencil body to contain the title and "edition" text. To add a graphic impact, I applied a Photoshop "Brush Strokes" filter named "Accented Edges."

After placing the three images, I made final layout and typography adjustments. The back cover and spine include the same elements. The spine uses only the pencil so it would be larger and more attention-getting on the bookstore shelf.

Original and modified versions of the pencil photo.

Other cover designs

The *Sweet Swan of Avon* cover includes a computer illustration I created with the natural-media paint tools in Corel Painter.

The *Macs on the Go* cover combines stock illustration from iStockPhoto.com (the globe) and typographic design.

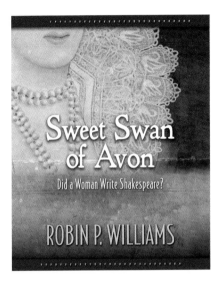

Who am I?

I'm really just a guy who always liked to draw. I have a Bachelor of Arts in Advertising Art from Louisiana College, a small private school in central Louisiana. I've co-authored more than a dozen books with Robin and designed all of the covers. I'm very jealous of contemporary designers because they never had to spec type, use rubber cement, or create comps with Magic Markers.

My professional background covers more than thirty years and various positions as art director, designer, and illustrator with a dozen advertising agencies, as a freelancer, and as a partner of a web development firm. Besides authoring books, I spend most of my time learning and teaching about digital creativity, videography, digital video editing, and podcasting.

The closest thing I have to a personal web site is UrlsInternetCafe.com. It's run by Url Ratz, a semi-famous, self-proclaimed Internet icon (shown below with pal Browser Nethound).

Words of wisdom

1) Develop a thick skin. When your design is rejected, don't dwell on it or take it personally. It's going to happen, no matter how good you are. And, more often than you think, it's going to give you the opportunity to create an even better design. If you can roll with the punches, you'll still be a designer ten years from now—and you'll be a lot better than you were ten years ago.

2) Approach design as a form of play. Explore and experiment. Amuse yourself. If you're having a good time, graphically speaking, other people will enjoy your work as well.

John Tollett
Graphic Designer

www.UrlsInternetCafe.com
jt@ratz.com

Harrah Lord
Book Designer

BOOK DESIGN FOR SELF-PUBLISHERS

I had been a designer for nearly fifteen years before I had the opportunity to start my own business and to focus on book design. Accidentally, and fortunately for me, I discovered there is a wonderful difference between producing books for publishers and "birthing" them with self-publishers. I appreciate the terrific relationships I have with the publishers I worked for, but I feel passionate about the relationships that develop with self-publishers.

Most of the courageous souls who have books in their hearts know little of what it takes to give them birth. They can be nervous and anxious; these are their "babies" they are trusting you with. I learned that developing a guide for the publishing process is essential—walking the self-publisher through the many steps involved, and explaining what they need to provide and when, helps them understand the time frame and what is required.

It also outlines what the designer is doing: managing the project; setting up a schedule and making sure deadlines are met; coordinating with the printer, editor/proofreader, and other resources; and helping them set a retail price. I have developed a detailed list of these steps to help guide those who require it (although most are satisfied with a simple explanation).

The part that many self-publishers don't think about is that once they have boxes and boxes of books in their guest room or garage, then they have to market and distribute the product of their labors. This is also something I was able to help with: pointing out the need for a web site and the importance

of creating a database of those who are interested in what they do; helping set up book signings; providing graphics to help promote the book; and making them aware of the extra amount of time and effort all this will take. Yes, after the "baby" is born, the author must "raise" it!

The following stories illustrate just of few of my favorite projects and the serendipitous ways a designer can find her clients.

Breakfast at the Inn

Hartstone Inn: Signature Recipes from an Elegant Maine Inn

My first experience with someone who wanted to self-publish was with Michael Salmon. He and his wife, Mary Jo, own a charming Victorian inn in Camden, Maine. I met Michael while taking one of his cooking classes. He mentioned that he was writing a cookbook and I suggested that he get in touch with a local publisher with whom I had just finished a cookbook. After a couple of months I received a call from him saying that the publisher didn't want to do what he wanted to do and that the editor thought I might be able to help him with his project.

This was exciting for me because it was my first opportunity to work with a person like this: someone with a vision, someone who loved his work, and someone who was also very easy to get along with. Michael had lined up a photographer (a student at the local photo workshop) and an editor (a frequent visitor to his inn). The former lived in Bermuda and the latter in NYC!

Michael was well-organized but didn't understand how a book came together. I walked him through the process: deciding on size, quantity, stock, and ink; choosing a printer and requesting quotes; selecting, ordering, and scanning images; and deciding on what other text to include besides recipes. We decided to print in Asia because we had the time (three months from when the final files are ready to go) and the cost, which including shipping, was less than if we printed in the States.

The book arrived in time for the summer season. By the end of the first year he had sold 2,500 of the 5,000 he had printed, thus recouping his expenses while promoting his inn and cooking classes. This summer we are doing a sequel.

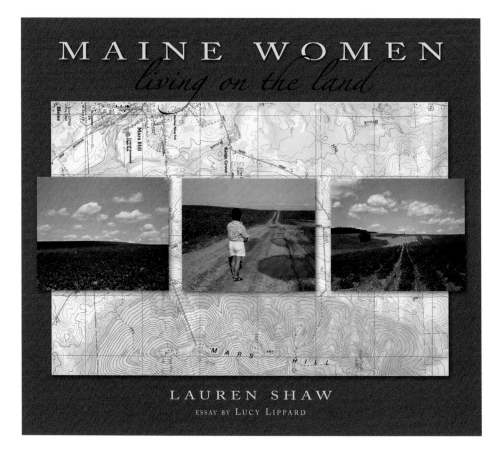

Maine Women:
Living on the Land

The Farnsworth Art Museum is a lovely jewel of a museum in Rockland, Maine, for whom I am lucky enough to have produced many exhibition catalogs. The curator told me they needed a DVD package plus a brochure for an upcoming photography exhibition. I went ahead and got quotes and did some preliminary designs. However, a couple of months later when I met with the curators and the photographer, Lauren Shaw from Boston, she asked me if it would be possible to create a book in time to accompany the exhibition.

This was May and the opening was early August. I promptly said, "Yes!" to her relief and excitement! She had the concept, knew the font she wanted, the text was written, the images were digital, and she had already decided on the order of their presentation. Having a book to accompany the DVD (the DVD was artfully inserted into a generous six-inch flap on the inside of the book) and the traveling exhibition offered something more tangible that people could view immediately. A DVD is wonderful— but you need equipment to view it!

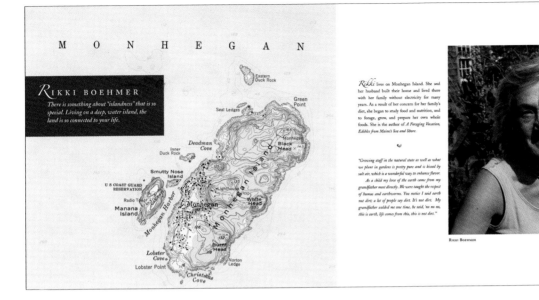

MONHEGAN

*R*IKKI BOEHMER

There is something about "islandness" that is so special. Living on a deep, water island, the land is so connected to your life.

Rikki lives on Monhegan Island. She and her husband built their home and lived there with her family without electricity for many years. As a result of her concern for her family's diet, she began to study food and nutrition, and to forage, grow, and prepare her own whole foods. She is the author of *A Foraging Vacation, Edibles from Maine's Sea and Shore.*

"Growing stuff in the natural state as well as what we plant in gardens is pretty pure and is kissed by salt air, which is a wonderful way to enhance flavor. As a child my love of the earth came from my grandfather most directly. We were taught the respect of humus and earthworms. You notice I said earth not dirt; a lot of people say dirt. It's not dirt. My grandfather scolded me one time, he said, 'no no no, this is earth, life comes from this, this is not dirt.'"

RIKKI BOEHMER

Getting to know and working with Lauren was amazing. Her project evolved over a nine-year period, during which she worked full-time as a professor at Emerson College. She traveled throughout Maine selecting, interviewing, and photographing ten incredible women who varied in age, location, occupation, and landscape— women who lead challenging lives on the land, successfully. Lauren gathered their stories and created an interactive DVD using stills, video, and voice-overs of the women speaking from their hearts.

The printing was very complicated; most of the images were duotones, but some were duotones combined with process color. To keep the costs down, I worked with the printer to make sure the process color images would be contained in one signature so the rest of the book could remain two-color. Even though the book was created in conjunction with the museum's exhibition, Lauren was paying for the printing costs.

So much is at stake for the self-publisher— the financial risk as well as the emotional. I believe the most important contribution I made (excluding the design and production and getting the book published on time) was being flexible, available, and patient. Listening to Lauren's concerns during many phone conversations helped her make informed decisions. Offering advice when needed, professional or friendly, was almost as necessary as my role as designer.

Creating this book with her was such an adventure—it has changed her life, and mine. After less than a year Lauren is ready to do a second printing, has turned a profit, and is on to her next project—we get to share in another adventure together!

Touchstones

I met Tillman and Donna Crane on a local open-studio tour in Maine. Tillman is a wonderfully sensitive and respected photographer specializing and teaching palladium print-making. I loved his prints, many of which were from his frequent trips to Scotland. They had already printed an impressive hardcover book of his work. His wife, Donna (a delightful and witty woman), runs the business out of their home while raising two kids and keeping Tillman on track. In the midst of our conversation I mentioned that I was a book designer and they told me they were thinking of doing another book . . .

The following year, Donna called and said they were ready. I learned that their first book project had been a disappointing experience and they wanted to do things very differently this time—they wanted fewer books, smaller in size, and they wanted to produce it locally. (The first book had been designed, produced, packaged, and printed in Italy; it had been very expensive and they had no input in the process.) So we sat down and went over all their concerns. We looked at many other books to get an idea of what they liked in a photography book, and we came up with the look they wanted: a fabric cover, the type foil-embossed, the image tipped in, inside a slip case. We discussed different printers and selected one in Vermont that was known for its care with photography books. The sales rep came to their studio and worked closely with us to achieve the right feel with paper and ink. Having someone to draw out and make tangible their vision was as important to them as being intimately involved in the process. By demystifying the language and explaining the pros and cons from a design viewpoint, they were able to make a number of concrete decisions from the beginning that saved them money.

For this book they decided on a limited print run of 500 with several packaging options, including signed and numbered photographic prints at different price points. Today, they have very few copies left, are preparing a sequel to this venture, and we are all looking forward to working together again.

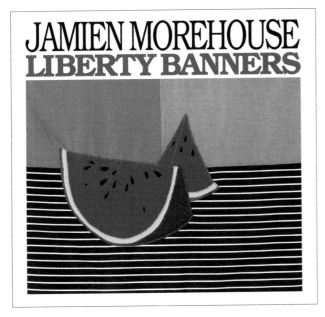

Jamien Morehouse: Liberty Banners

Through my connections with the Farnsworth Art Musuem, I was asked to work on a retrospective of Jamien Morehouse's banner art. Jamien was a woman who passed away in her 48th year from breast cancer in 1999. She left behind a husband, four sons, parents, and a community that stretched far and wide.

She also left a legacy of making a difference in every life she touched—and multitudes of banners which still unfurl in the wind after nearly thirty years. Several of her good friends and one of her sons, Sam, a senior in college, got the idea to have an exhibition of her banners and create a book documenting their importance in her life and the lives of many others.

The project was unique for me because I would be working with a project manager (a woman whom I had worked with before and liked very much) and the son. They had the monumental task of locating the banners and photographing them, finding old photographs of when they were first made and scanning them, and digitally enhancing color where possible. My role was to instruct Sam about book production, produce the layout, and guide his creative vision so it landed on the pages of the book in a timely manner. He had excellent graphic sense and creative ideas which I supported and worked with. This required flexibility, patience, and no ego!

In the end, the book arrived on time for the exhibition's reception. Everyone was touched by what it said and revealed about this amazing woman—and her son. I believe this endeavor brought much healing to her family and friends, as well as honor to her memory and art. I was thankful to have been a part of this.

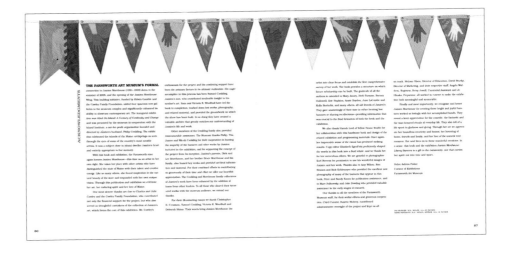

The 11 Intentions:
Invoking the Sacred Feminine
as a Pathway to Inner Peace

Finally, I need to mention my experience with print-on-demand for the self-publisher.

I "met" Lynda Terry while we were both working together on a completely different book—she as editor/proofreader and me as design/production person; she in California, me in Maine. As we were working, she mentioned that she had just completed a book of her own and was planning on printing it with Lulu.com, a POD (print-on-demand) service. This venue enabled her to print a small run, 150 copies, with less of an initial expense than printing with offset. She would get her book "out there," see how it was received, and then hopefully go back and print 500–1000 if the the reception was favorable.

Most POD services offer cover design for a modest fee (often resulting in a "modest" design). Terry and her husband decided to make the extra investment to hire a designer. Since she and I had worked well together on other projects and she liked my design style, we teamed up. Her book was text-only so it lent itself well to the POD format. The web site gives explicit instructions, which are quite different from those for offset, and is prompt with their tech support.

She had her books in hand within the month, was very pleased with the results, and was on the road promoting it the following months. We still have never met but have shared personal aspects of our lives, encouraged one another, and hope to meet someday! AND, I have received two requests from other women who want to self-publish after seeing how Lynda's book came out.

Who am I?

I found graphic design late in life. I managed to graduate from college with a B.A. in Art History and Psychology and then went on to be a lousy fashion model, a successful men's clothing designer, a doting single mom, a miserable bank teller, a bored seismic analyst, a Kelly Girl who couldn't type, and an amazed graphic design student at the local community college—finally discovering something that I really liked to do and could do it fairly well—all in that order.

After eight years of being the art director for a small publishing company in California, I moved east, back to my New England roots, and began my own book design business. Perfect timing: DSL, UPS/FedEx, and almost everyone connected via email made it possible for me to live my dream of working for myself, at home, in an out-of-the-way gorgeous locale. The second best thing I ever did. The first best thing I ever did was being brave and blessed enough to birth and raise a fabulous son who has just become a husband and a father, and is still the apple of my eye!

Words of wisdom

What is typical about working with self-publishers is that it requires trust between the client and the designer; intuitive listening skills to "hear" the voice of the client; the ability to capture their vision in their book via all the aspects that go into it (paper, ink, size, graphics, layout, binding); flexibility; and the willingness to be deeply involved for months with someone, being in their life, sharing this exciting part of their journey. A rewarding partnership.

But other than that, each project is delightfully different because of the uniqueness of the writer/artist/photographer/chef and what they have to offer the world.

All my life I have received great joy in helping others achieve their dreams and now I have found a wonderful vehicle to realize my dream as well. I will probably never get rich (quick or slow), but I am exceedingly prosperous in the relationships I have formed and the experiences I have shared with these truly remarkable people.

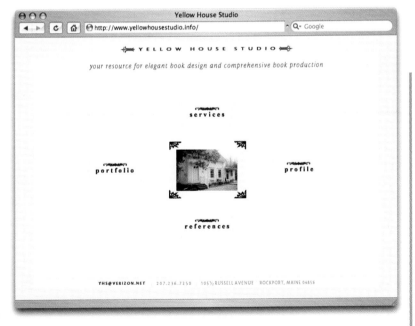

Harrah Lord
Yellow House Studio
105½ Russell Avenue
Rockport, Maine
04856

207 236 7250 *phone*

YHS@verizon.net
www.YellowHouseStudio.info

Brian Forstat
Web Design & Development

WEB SITE DESIGN AND DEVELOPMENT

AgilityGraphics.com portfolio site

The purpose of this web site was to show potential employers who I was and some of the work I had done.

My goal was to create a web site that was clean and elegant, a bit techie, and mainly focused on my work. I wanted the site to be both visually as well as technically exciting, yet in a very minimal manner. I was aware that the results of what I wanted to do, in terms of development, would probably be missed by most viewers because I was not going for intricate animations and such, but rather ActionScript-driven functionality without all the flashiness.

I love Flash and believe my Flash skills are one of my stronger assets, so I wanted to work show this dynamically. I wanted the site to be focused on the work and avoid as much waiting as possible. At the time I was building the site, I was interested in the capabilities of Flash as a tool to build practical web sites, but ones that don't necessarily have all the Flash characteristics we are used to, such as animation, sound, and video. I was intrigued by Flash sites that didn't use major timelines. My goal was to try to keep timelines non-existent or to a minimum by using ActionScript for any of the interactivity and events.

I was building the site with the intention of getting a job with a design firm in San Francisco, where I had just moved. My target audience for this site was interactive design agencies; I assumed that the people I was hoping to work for would have the latest player installed because it's their job to stay current.

I worked with the new (at the time) Flash 8 format. I wanted to work with the Flash 8 plugin because it allowed me to make use of the new plugin detection behavior, as well as the much improved text rendering which made it possible to use smaller non-Flash fonts in my design.

Another thing I wanted to do in this site was make it a full-browser Flash site, which is a site that fills the whole browser regardless of how big it is.

I created all the main content in a MovieClip, which would keep it top- and center-aligned. I prevented the content from scaling so loaded images would not become pixelated. I also created a little peel-off corner that would always sit in the bottom-left of the screen.

Since this site was for myself, I had no one telling me what to do or how to do it. This made the process a bit different from designing for a client—I did not design several comps to show to the client, but had design sessions with myself where I just experimented and did what I wanted or thought might work.

I had actually started this project several times and abandoned the comps I had done. There were many different ways I could have taken my site's direction and at first I was not quite sure which way to go. It is harder sometimes to design your own web site then it is to do work for other people. You have to decide how you want other people to perceive you, which is hard when you realize that it might determine whether or not you will ever meet them or get the job. I know quite a few designers who struggle most with work they do for themselves. I think we tend to become overly critical of our own work—to the point where the process can get stagnant. In my case, a friend of mine designed and built his site in two weeks and that really put me in check. I made the decision to "just get it done" even if it didn't turn out to be "the best thing I have ever worked on."

One important thing I had learned from my last web site is that I wanted to have a site that was about quality rather than quantity. I wanted to show my most current and best work and have control over what the viewer would see. A viewer will only spend so much time on your site, and rather than give them an overwhelming number of pieces to look at, I would limit the options to make sure they would see what I want them to see. I also wanted to be able to update the site frequently and easily.

If I had to do this project again today, I would probably do some things quite a bit differently, but by doing it this way I learned a great deal.

Banyan Wines web site

www.BanyanWines.com

My good friend Kenny Likitprakong, a winemaker in California, asked me to build a site for one of his side projects, a wine label called **Banyan Wines.** Banyan Wines produces white wines from sustainable or organic grape sources, with Asian food pairing in mind. The initial idea was to build a simple and elegant web site to introduce the wine and give viewers a place to find information about the wines and the company.

In our initial meeting, Kenny made it clear that he wanted me to take the initiative in terms of the look and feel. Together we figured out what sections the site should include and talked a bit about direction, imagery, and site behavior. I designed three comps for the first round, two of which were our favorites. After

showing those to a couple of other friends, we decided on one. I took that comp and worked on it for another round, making some minor changes and designing the secondary pages. Kenny was extremely easy to work with, a combination of his easy-going attitude and his trust in my ability.

What we had designed was quite a bit different from what most winery web sites were looking like at the time. Kenny was hoping to visually differentiate himself from the rest of the field, representing the new generation of wine makers. Many of the other winery sites had either plain, low-tech HTML pages or cartoon-style, illustration Flash sites. Banyan saw itself differently.

Once we had figured out the design, the development was smooth. The idea was to have everything move fluidly and from one section to the next without any abrupt changes. The site was published in an early version of Flash; each section's behaviors are inside an MC, whose timeline triggers the ActionScripts at the appropriate time. All tweens are done with ActionScript on the root timeline.

I have probably received more positive response for this project than any other site I've done. If I had to do this one again today, I would do some things differently in the development, but it was a great stepping stone for my education in Flash and ActionScript-driven tweens.

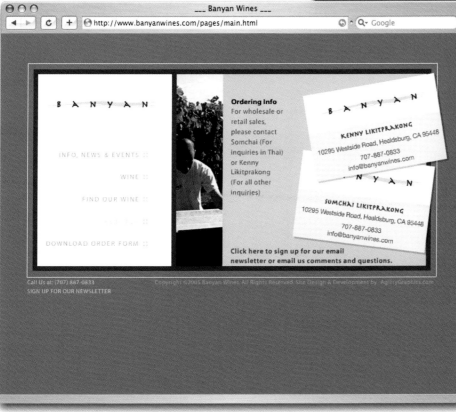

PMuck web site
www.PMuck.de

My good friend Philipp Muckenfuss, who lives in Germany, is a digital music producer. I had previously built him a temporary web site. His album was about to be released and the temporary site was no longer enough.

The first web site had been a one-page site; we liked it that way and decided to stay with that idea. His album had already been designed, so we decided to use some of the elements from it as the look-and-feel-for the new web site.

The challenge was that all of the design elements had been created to work on the cover of a record sleeve, which has four defined edges. It used organic things such as leaves, sticks, garbage, old rusted objects, as well as masking tape and duct tape.

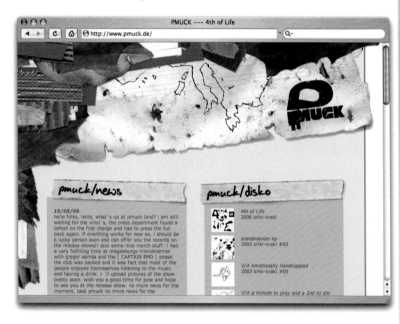

I wanted the web site to be consistent with the record sleeve. The challenge was to take design elements from the record sleeve, which were all cropped in weird ways to work within the square shape of the package, and build them into the context of the web site. I wanted it to look a bit like these things were thrown on the pages, organically placed in the space available, with no cut-off edges on any of the objects.

For this project, I ended up working in Photoshop for quite some time. I wanted the whole thing to look somewhat natural, which meant, for example, that the masking tape, which looks like it's peeling in some places, needed custom shadows for each piece. The same was true for the grunged-out areas of the text boxes, etc. I wanted each one to look different. This in turn, created a new challenge—to build the site efficiently and save bandwidth where possible, since all these images and all the content on a one-page design were adding weight to the download.

One other thing I had to consider was that most of the content was stuff that would change frequently. Since I did not want to rebuild every time things were changing, I needed to create a design that would adjust automatically to changes. All content was placed in "boxes"—which I built with CSS to expand and contract with the amount of content in them. This way, all of the content "boxes" have the same amount of padding around their content and are all different in length.

Because some of the content was too long, as in the case of the news "box," I used CSS to create a scrollable area and set it to a specific height.

Mary Sidney web site
www.MarySidney.com

Robin had asked if I wanted to design a web site for one of the books she was working on and I was excited about the opportunity. The site was for her book *Sweet Swan of Avon: Did a Woman Write Shakespeare?*, in which she researched the possibility that the plays and sonnets attributed to William Shakespeare were actually written by a woman.

The design idea was to create a very clean and elegant site that was easy to navigate and well organized. We needed to present a relatively large amount of information to people generally interested in the book or the topic. My goal in designing for this web site was to try to keep the design light enough so the large amount of text on some pages would not seem like a deterrent to some of the viewers.

The concept that we finally chose was quite a simple one in terms of its appearance—lots of white space with rather minimal visual elements at the top of each page. I used a three-column design with the navigation in the first column, content in the middle, and quotes or other interesting information on the right.

The site is a tableless CSS design. The navigation is also CSS and uses the same rollover image for each button. Using older technology, this kind of navigation would have created a longer download; using CSS, it becomes extremely quick and efficient. It also ensures that the navigation and the body copy will always use the same font.

Who am I?

I am a freelance web designer and developer, graphic designer, and photographer. Born, raised, and educated in Germany, I moved to California in 1996 for college and now permanently reside in San Francisco.

The first extended period of time I spent in the U.S. was in 1992/93 as a foreign exchange student in Santa Rosa, California. I was extremely lucky to get placed with the family of Robin Williams and her kids, Ryan, Jimmy, and Scarlett. At the time, I thought computers were for geeks and really did not want to have anything to do with them. I would see Robin work 18-hour days for weeks at a time and found it hard to believe that anyone would want to do that.

Staying with Robin for that year was probably one of the most wonderful, exciting, and life-changing experiences of my life and I am grateful for her support. She has always been extremely encouraging, trusting, and helpful with anything I talked to her about and continues to be like that to this day. I am certain that if it was not for that year staying with Robin and her kids, my life would be extremely different today.

I have always been interested in design in various forms and have been designing for print and web since 1999. I have worked in-house as well as freelance, working with both large and small clients.

Since 2003 my main focus has been on freelance, working with my own clients, as well as assisting several design firms in the San Francisco Bay Area with their design, development, and production needs.

I enjoy what I do and plan to keep learning and growing to further my career, whatever that might be. I like that there is always something new to try and learn, as doing tedious tasks can drive me crazy at times . . . .

Words of wisdom

Be nice to your clients and coworkers and they will be nice to you (most of the time anyway). A lot of people are good at what they do, and that's a prerequisite to being successful, but in the end, people want to work with people they like, trust, and enjoy interacting with.

Brian Forstat
Agility Graphics
San Francisco, California

415 386 1142 *phone*

www.AgilityGraphics.com
brian@AgilityGraphics.com

www.TonalClothing.com
info@TonalClothing.com

Carmen Sheldon
Graphic Design Instructor

COLLEGE INSTRUCTOR OF GRAPHIC DESIGN

Applied Graphics Program
Students' projects

The Applied Graphics program at Santa Rosa Junior College, California, is designed to provide the student entry-level skills for business or industry. The program delivers a practical hands-on experience in graphic fundamentals such as design, layout techniques, computer applications, illustration, multimedia, digital production techniques, offset printing, and business practices. The students spend much of their time creating practical design pieces from initial concept all the way through final digital output.

This is the program Robin graduated from in 1980 (pre-computer); eventually she started running the program and taught the core first-year curriculum. She and Carmen met at SRJC in 1978 and have been close friends and partners ever since.

This section displays several of Carmen's design projects with her advanced students.

Student specs: Tea Box Case Study

Ms. Hempleworth is opening a tea room in downtown Sonoma [California], right on the square. She has leased a charming, newly remodeled space. She wants to play into the bucolic feeling of the Sonoma area and so she has named her new little business *Ewe and Me Tea Room*. She will be serving a traditional high tea with all the ceremony. However, she wants to be sure her business has a variety of services to offer her customers, so in addition to a little tea shop where she will sell gifts and a variety of gourmet teas, a bakery, and a catering service, she wants to offer boxed, picnic tea fare.

She would like you to design her tea boxes. She wants a soft, charming, but not too "cutsie" look. The concept must include a stylized image of a sheep. She doesn't want men to feel out of place by having the box seem too feminine.

Her boxes will hold two scones, four little sandwiches, two tarts, two tiny napkins, a small jar of jam, several pats of butter, and two packages of tea. She certainly wants her box to say "delicious food" so it shouldn't look like a retail gift box.

You may consider any approach with the provided white box—a band around the box, an all-over design, a typographic look, whatever you feel might suit Ms. Hempleworth.

My Thoughts

This is a great project because I only allow the students about four hours to come up with concepts and complete their comps. The students walk into the classroom cold with no prior knowledge of what they will be working on. I then produce a bag, box, candy bar, bottle, whatever it is that day, and have them develop a design. This method requires the students to think on their feet and work very quickly. I do several of these "case studies" every semester and although the students panic at first, they soon learn to love the pace and are usually surprised that they can come up with a viable idea in that small amount of time. In fact, one of my students said, "Can we do more case studies; this is so much fun!" I often find that the students even feel their case study designs are stronger than ones they work with for weeks. The immediacy and the fact that they have to make quick decisions teaches good discipline and a realistic preparation for the world of graphic design.

Credits clockwise: Yvone Whang, Molly Cushman, Audrey Sculley

credits left to right: Yvone Wang, Leah Anderson, Darrell Perry, Kathleen Blair, Rebecca Parola, Terry McDonough

Student specs: Wine Label Project

We live in the wine country so we have to design a wine label. They are just too beautiful to ignore and there is a lot we can learn about specialty printing techniques. You are to create a fictitious winery and design a label for it. If you look at a lot of label designs you will find that many labels concentrate on typography so this should be addressed very carefully in your design.

> The emphasis of the project is concept. Really do some brainstorming and research. You are creating the total package so pay attention to the foils, neck labels, back labels, etc.

> Typography must be an important part of your design.

> Include a specialty technique such as emboss, hot foil stamp, die cut, etc.

> Pay attention to the "legals."

> You may decide the size. Watch how it fits the bottle. Also, find out what types of wine go in which bottles— don't embarrass yourself.

> Submit computer color output.

> Present your label in a pocket on a presentation board.

> Hand in computer-generated color separations on 8.5" x 11" transparency material.

credits left to right: Jason Hill, Jackie Mujica, David Berg, Claudia Strijek, Julie Cook

My Thoughts

Nothing beats success. The students really enjoy this project because it looks stunning upon completion. Although my students don't run right out and start designing wine labels after two years of a community college graphic design program, they do get a lot of positive feedback from their labels. It gives them a chance to work with image, color and type—aspects of most visual communication pieces. It makes them really hone their designs because the format doesn't allow for unnecessary elements. It is a good lesson for all the principles because the format is so restricted. All the contrast, proximity, and alignment issues become very apparent.

I never allow my students to head for the computer without working out their designs in thumbnail form. I want them to think before they get too filter-drop-shadow-twirl-tool happy. They hate it, but their work is better because of it.

259

Credits left to right: Barb Wendel, Terry McDonough, Jeanne Thomas, Kim Reid, Linda Palo, Donna Mathis

My Thoughts

I like this project because it really lets the students explore their creativity and have some fun. Oh, sure, some of these designs go way over the top—to produce them in the real world of print production would probably bankrupt the client—but we do our share of budget-driven projects and this one allows the students to really stun each other with their whimsical creativity.

The students work in pairs, playing the parts of both designer and client. This does make them stretch as often the student partial to hard rock must design a cover for classical strings.

There are a lot of "real world" graphics that play a part in this project as the students must create a sizable folded insert complete with photos, song lyrics, and type treatments. I also insist that they separate their computer files.

Student specs: CD Project

A new and upcoming musical group needs you to design a promotional CD for their group. This is not only the retail packaging for the CD but also a "promo," a 3D ad designed to get the radio station's attention. In this project you get the chance to work with a "designer." You will be split up in pairs and each of you will get the chance to be the "client" and "designer." You will provide each other with the name of the musical group, the type of music, and your personal preferences concerning design.

› The emphasis of the project is concept. Really do some brainstorming and research.

› Include type on the label of the CD.

› Include a fold-out with information on the group or song lyrics.

› Submit computer color output.

› Present your piece in a protective box.

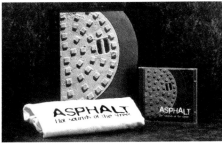

Credits left to right: Patrice Morris, Lisa Howard, Linda Palo, Molly Cushman

Words of Wisdom

Never let the computer design for you. Your mind, experiences, perceptions, and knowledge are the best tools for coming up with visual communications that really matter. Draw some scribbles on a scrap of paper. Think! Look! Go for a walk! Collect leaves! Take a photo of a river rock. Pick up a feather. Then turn on your computer.

Who am I?

After graduating with a degree in Advertising Design from Pacific Union College, Robin and I started our own design studio, The Double Image. Of course, we had to learn the business end by the seat of our pants, but we had lots of fun creating logos, ads, and brochures for the local businesses. I do think we spent most of our profits on truffles, Oreo cookies, and silkscreen ink for our beautiful serigraphs. After working in several different design capacities, I eventually started teaching in the Applied Graphics Program at Santa Rosa Junior College. I found my niche: I could share my passion for design and also tie into that streak of altruism that's in my bones from being a "missionary kid." I love my students and get great satisfaction out of seeing them bloom from tentative amateurs into confident design professionals.

Carmen Sheldon
Santa Rosa Junior College
Applied Graphics Program
1501 Mendocino Avenue
Santa Rosa, California
95401

707 527 4909 *phone*

csheldon@santarosa.edu
www.SantaRosa.edu/aptech/

John Burns

Lettering Artist

CUSTOM LETTERFORM DESIGN

When asked what I do for a living, I say, "I designed the 'Ruffles' brand—not the whole package, just the lettering. I also did 'Sara Lee', 'Baby Ruth', and 'Intel Inside.'" That usually leads to a conversation about the fact that within the field of graphic design, I operate in a very narrow niche—custom letterform design. If you think about the packages in a grocery store, how many of them use a typeface for their brand? Very few, right? My job is to create those custom brands. And, no, I don't get royalties for each bag of Ruffles sold. But thanks for asking.

Professional lettering is similar to illustration, in that I do most of my work for art directors in design firms and advertising agencies. Such companies rarely have staff lettering artists, so I am hired on a project basis. I have a home office and I work with designers all over the country. Every project begins with a briefing from the art director. We discuss the product and who will be buying it. I ask for adjectives describing the attributes they want the package to convey. At this point, some designers give very specific direction, referencing samples from my web site. Others are less comprehensive. One designer simply said, "Just be brilliant."

Client: Oscar V. Mulder
Proposed identity for a line of health supplements

Client: Lipson, Alport & Glass Associates
Proposed Lipton Tea Brand

Creating letters

The field of lettering can be generally broken down into two camps: drawn (or built-up) letterforms and calligraphic letterforms. Drawn letterforms most often begin as pencil sketches. Outlines are drawn, and the letters are filled in. Calligraphic letterforms are made with single strokes by such tools as broad-edged pens and pointed brushes. With rare exceptions, all letterforms (including typefaces) are begun by hand. Computers are used in later stages as finalizing tools.

To give an edginess to the Ravens identity, every shape (except for the tennis ball) was created using straight lines.

Identity for a tennis team

Starting with type

My clients want identity solutions that are ownable, or "proprietary" (as it is called), a logotype that can't be simply typed out using an existing font. So what I do regularly involves some amount of custom handling. But sometimes I start with a typeface as the basis of my design. Adobe Illustrator allows you to type words, then convert the letters into editable points, thereby providing a perfect start for customization.

An experimental theater group

Three Helvetica fonts were used as a starting point for the Rabble Fish Theater identity. The custom work came in altering parts of the letters, to allow them to nest and fit well together.

The Office Power logotype was created with the typeface Futura. The cap "P" was then redrawn so the plug could be carved out of the negative space.

Client: The Thompson Design Group
Proposed identity for a line of office electrical accessories

GOODSTART

*Client: Colemanbrandworx
Proposed identity for a
Nestlé formula product*

*Initial caps, type on a curve, swash strokes, ligatures
and little cut-in shapes combine to make this treatment
of Good Start ownable. Note that all of those devices
are not found in a standard typeface, which gives you
a key for developing a proprietary design.*

Type-like letterforms from scratch

The Harp identity is based on non-specific sans serif letter-forms. The curved extensions of the letters give the design motion, unity, and a proprietary feel.

Calligraphic letterforms

Each part of a calligraphic letterform is executed with a single stroke. Therefore, the curves and shapes of the letters are determined by the tool used to create them.

The Meadowood identity (below) and the Mary Sidney Society identity (top of the next page) were created with a broad-edged marker, or, what most people would call a "calligraphy pen." The thicks and thins are created by holding the marker at a consistent angle while drawing the letters. To create the rough edges of the Mary Sidney identity, the lettering was done on watercolor paper.

*Client: Primo Angeli, Inc.
Proposed identity for a Guinness lager*

*Client: Chuck House
Proposed identity for a luxury resort*

264

Client: Mary Sidney Society
A non-profit organization that
honors "unsung women."

Mary **SIDNEY** SOCIETY

Taste Experience

Client: Aurora Group
Proposed identity for a culinary website

The letters to the left and below were all created with a pointed brush. It's a remarkably versatile tool, allowing you to create the thicks and thins of the letters by applying varying pressure. The rough texture of the "Friends of Calligraphy" letters were created by lettering with black ink on watercolor paper. The art was later retouched, scanned, and reversed out of the black box.

Friends of Calligraphy

Directory cover art for a San Francisco–based calligraphy organization

Popfit

Client: Lipson, Alport & Glass Associates

Making letters digital

Virtually all graphic communications end up in a digital form, so I always supply my final art in digital form. For letters that have a textured edge, I scan the art as a TIFF file, then convert it to vector art using Streamline software (in the pre-OS X days) or the Live Trace option in Illustrator CS2. For letter-forms that need a smooth edge, auto-tracing is not precise enough, so I scan my sketches as TIFF or PICT files, place them on a template layer in Illustrator, then redraw them using the pen tool.

Client: Britton Design
Proposed identity for a winery

Client: McLean Design

All of the samples on this page were created with a Ruling Writer,™ an updated version of the ruling pen. Depending on the pressure applied, the angle you hold the tool, and the paper used, you can achieve a variety of looks and textures. I have a certain lack of control when using this tool, and I like that. It leads to some happy accidents.

Client: Lipson, Alport & Glass Associates
Proposed Tropicana product

Proposed identity for an international calligraphy conference

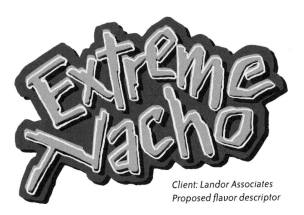

Client: Landor Associates
Proposed flavor descriptor

The capabilities of Adobe Illustrator have made it easier to create art like Extreme Nacho, above. The base (orange) letters were drawn by hand, scanned, and converted to outline. Then, the rest was created using copied and stroked versions of that art. Additional dimensionalizing effects could be added using Photoshop filters, but if the brand is to be used in a range of sizes, art directors prefer vector art because of its scalability.

And in the end...

"As Creative As U Wanna B" was an exercise in integrating positive and negative shapes to create letters. This design was worked out with pencil and marker on many sheets of tracing paper, then the final was done with the pen tool in Illustrator.

Call-for-entries identity for The Sadies, the annual award show of the Sonoma County Ad Club in California.

Who am I?

I earned a BFA in Graphic Design from Carnegie-Mellon University, then immediately became a professional actor. (Not all career paths are straight lines.) During days, I wrote songs and designed comps for Broadway show posters.

Next came positions as a magazine art director and in-house graphic designer, where I realized that letterforms, typography, and calligraphy are my real passion.

When I'm not working, you'll probably find me on a tennis court.

Words of wisdom

I once took a workshop on discovering one's gifts, and I'm going to tell you about the most important exercise in the workshop. Make a list of the things you're really good at, starting with what you do best. Right next to that, make a list of the things you most like to do. Anything that shows up close to the top of both lists is a gift. So now, make your lists, then go out and use your gifts!

John Burns
John Burns Lettering and Design

www.JohnBurnsLettering.com

words of wisdom

"Don't Be a Wimp!"

"TAKE THE TIME TO UNDERSTAND YOUR AUDIENCE."

"BE NICE."

"GO USE YOUR gift"

"Think and sketch before you turn on the computer."

"Don't be afraid of an idea."

"DEVELOP A THICK SKIN"

"Be deeply involved."

"Simply be aware. Of everything."

"Know why you're doing what you're doing."

EXTRAS

Fonts in this book

All fonts are shown at 12 point

Classic Sans Serif

Alinea Sans

Antique Olive Light to **Nord**

Avant Garde

Bailey Sans family

Charlotte Sans Book, **Bold,** SMALL CAPS

Frutiger Light, *Light Italic,* **Black, UltraBlack**

Futura Condensed Light

Helvetica

Humana Sans Light, *Light Italic,* **Bold**

Officina Sans family, **Extra Bold, Black**

Myriad Pro family

Today Sans Bold

Trade Gothic Light, *Light Oblique,* **Bold, Bold Condensed**

Univers Roman, Condensed, Condensed Light, **Bold, Condensed Bold**

VAG Rounded Thin, Light, **Bold, Black**

Decorative Sans Serif

Barmeno Extra Bold

Blur Light, **Medium, Bold**

Bodega Sans Light, **Medium, Black**

BroadBand

Highlander Book

HUXLEY VERTICAL

MACHINE

PLanet Sans Book, **Bold**

SERENGETTI

Tempus Sans

Wade Sans Light

Hybrid Sans/Serif

Dyadis Book, SMALL CAPS, **Bold,** *Bold Italic*

Gilgamesh, *Italic,* **Bold,** SMALL CAPS

Senator Tall

SevenSerif, **Black**

Decorative

Airstream

Alleycat

Amoebia Rain

BEE/KNEE/

Bossa Nova

CANCIONE

CONFIDENTIAL

DYNAMOE

FLOWERCHILD

GARISHMONDE

Green Plain

hanzel

Impakt

Industria Solid, Inline, Industria Solid A

Industrial Heavy, Plain

Kumquat

Litterbox

Musica

Out of the Fridge

Pious Henry

PLanet Serif, SMALL CAPS DEMI

Schmutz Cleaned

Silvermoon, Bold

Smack

SOPHIA

Stoclet Light, **Bold**

THE WALL

Toontime

Tree Boxelder, Monkey Puzzle, Persimmon

Woodland Light, **Heavy**

Zanzibar ❧

Script

Bellevue

Bickham Script Pro (this is 18 point)

Caflish Script Pro

Carpenter

Dartangnon

Dear Sarah

Dorchester

Hollyweird

Linoscript

Mistral

Redonda Fancy

Shelley Volante

Signature

Spring Regular and Light

Zaragoza

Classic Serif

Adobe Garamond, *Italic,* **Bold,** ***Bold Italic***

Adobe Caslon, EXPERT

Bell, *Italic*

Berkeley

Centaur, *Italic,* **Bold**

Clarendon, Light, **Bold**

Clearface, *Italic*

Cochin, *Italic*

CRESCI

Galliard, *Italic,* **Black**

Golden Cockerel, *Italic, Ornaments*

Cheltenham family

Garamond Light (ITC), **Bold,** ***Bold Italic***

Giovanni, *Italic*

Meridien, *Italic*

Palatino, *Italic*

Times

TopHat, *Italic*

TRAJAN

Walbaum, *Italic*

Moderns

AT Quirnus Bold

Craw Modern

Fenice Light, **Ultra**

Firenze

MAGNOLIA

Onyx

Picture fonts, clip art fonts

Art Three:

Backyard Beasties :

Bill's Modern Diner:

Birds:

Diva Doodles:

DFSituations One (ITC):

DFSituations Two (ITC):

Fontoonies (ITC):

Gargoonies (ITC):

MiniPics Confetti:

MiniPics Head Buddies:

Renfields Lunch:

Type Embellishments One, Two, and Three:

Zapf Dingbats:

Many thanks to **Veer.com** for their cooperation and generosity as we worked on the creation of this book. Their fantastic and varied selection of fonts, stock images, and clip art were used in many of the design examples and were also used to illustrate many of the editorial pages of this book. Their products provided compelling imagery and a great amount of inspiration.

Some of the Veer collections we used include Digital Vision, ObjectGear, Circa:Art, Art Parts, DataStorm, Business Edge, ArtVille, and others.

Special thanks to the incredible **iStockPhoto.com** site for an affordable resource for stock images! And many thanks for the borders and frames from **Aridi.com** and **AutoFX.com**.

And huge thanks to Brian Forstat (AgilityGraphics.com) and Landon Dowlen (Landonsea. com), a couple of great young designers, for contributing some of the graphics and web sites; to Linda Johnson of Swell Design for her beautiful brochure design; to DNAcommunications.com, RothRitter.com, and L Studio.net for allowing us to showcase some of their web sites!

273

Index

Two pages for you to Doodle in!